# Sex and Sexuality in Tudor England

# Sex and Sexuality in Tudor England

Carol McGrath

PEN & SWORD
HISTORY

First published in Great Britain in 2022 by
Pen & Sword History
An imprint of
Pen & Sword Books Ltd
Yorkshire – Philadelphia

ISBN 978 1 52676 918 3

A CIP catalogue record for this book is
available from the British Library.

Typeset by Mac Style
Printed and bound in the UK by CPI Group (UK) Ltd,
Croydon, CR0 4YY.

MIX
Paper from
responsible sources
FSC® C013604

Pen & Sword Books Limited incorporates the imprints of Atlas,
Archaeology, Aviation, Discovery, Family History, Fiction, History,
Maritime, Military, Military Classics, Politics, Select, Transport,
True Crime, Air World, Frontline Publishing, Leo Cooper, Remember
When, Seaforth Publishing, The Praetorian Press, Wharncliffe
Local History, Wharncliffe Transport, Wharncliffe True Crime
and White Owl.

For a complete list of Pen & Sword titles please contact

PEN & SWORD BOOKS LIMITED
47 Church Street, Barnsley, South Yorkshire, S70 2AS, England
E-mail: enquiries@pen-and-sword.co.uk
Website: www.pen-and-sword.co.uk

Or

PEN AND SWORD BOOKS
1950 Lawrence Rd, Havertown, PA 19083, USA
E-mail: Uspen-and-sword@casematepublishers.com
Website: www.penandswordbooks.com

*For Yvonne*

# Contents

# Introduction

On a Monday morning of 13 February 1542, Katherine Howard, fifth wife of Henry VIII, first cousin to Anne Boleyn, young, vivacious, and captivating stepped, assisted, onto the scaffold, pale and terrified. In menacing manner, the Tower of London loomed up behind her. She had not been kept prisoner on the night prior to her execution in the queen's apartments within the Tower itself as they were being refurbished but instead in a recently built house overlooking the green.

Katherine had, according to legend, passed the previous night practising laying her head upon the block. Shivering on the scaffold, she asked forgiveness for her sins, acknowledging she deserved to die a thousand deaths for betraying the King who had treated her most graciously. Katherine, whom Henry had called 'the very jewel of womanhood' was subsequently beheaded with just one stroke of the axe. After her death, Francis I of France wrote a letter to King Henry regretting 'the lewd and naughty [evil] behaviour of the Queen,' advising Henry that the 'lightness of women cannot bend to the honour of men.'

What had occurred to bring this girl, still in her teens, to such a horrible end?

During the Northern Progress of 1541 Katherine's personal behaviour was questioned and a storm around her broke soon afterwards. It was suggested she was involved with Thomas Culpepper, a young man whom she had considered marrying during her time as maid of honour to Anne of Cleves, Henry's fourth wife. It was alleged that after her marriage to Henry, the Queen and Culpepper had met secretly, their meetings arranged by her senior lady-in-waiting, Jane Boleyn, widow of Katherine's executed cousin, George Boleyn. Too many people knew about her past. Lady Rochford talked after Mary Lascelles revealed how she had observed the 'light' ways of Queen Katherine at Lambeth while she was a ward. Mary Lascelles revealed that Katherine had experienced earlier sexual behaviour with Francis Dereham, a member of her step-grandmother's household. Katherine Howard may have entered into this alliance in good faith, hand-fasting herself to Dereham. They exchanged promises and gifts. They spent nights in a shared bed in the young ladies' dormitory as husband and wife and during investigations into her past it was reported 'they hung together by the belly like sparrows.'

An enquiry led by the Archbishop of Canterbury, Thomas Cranmer, scrutinised Mary Lascelles' revelations. Yet the archbishop had his own motivation because Protestant Cramner hoped to use the Queen's indiscretions to topple the Roman Catholic 'Norfolk' family to which Katherine belonged. Henry himself never knew of the allegations until 1 November, All Saints' Day, 1541, when a warrant for the Queen's arrest describing her crimes was slipped to him while he was at Mass. Henry was devastated. As more evidence was revealed, including a love letter scribed in her own hand and discovered in Culpepper's chamber, Katherine became more and more distraught. She was questioned by Archbishop Cranmer and, out of her wits with fear, confessed to her liaison with Culpepper.

This tragic sad story, not the first attached to King Henry's queens, tells of the ultimate penalty suffered by a young girl in love accused of 'light' behaviour that suggested adultery. It illustrates the dangers of romantic love during this era and speaks of the ultimate price paid by a very young queen for forbidden sex. The early sixteenth century was a time when adultery was overheard through keyholes and windows. It was an era when people lived in close proximity, even a queen, and it was difficult to keep personal lives private. The Tudor period was one in which a whistle-blowing society excelled and it could be exceptionally vicious. Nothing could long remain secret.

*    *    *

The Tudor Era for the purposes of this book begins in 1485 and ends with the accession of Queen Elizabeth I to the throne in 1558. We date it back to 1485 when Henry VIII's father, Henry VII, defeated the last Plantagenet king, Yorkist Richard III on Bosworth Field, ending the Cousins' War between the Houses of Lancaster and York. The new Tudor dynasty was cemented by the arranged regal marriage between

Henry VII of Lancaster and Elizabeth of York, daughter of Yorkist king, Edward IV.

Many beliefs concerning sex and sexuality did not change significantly with the advent of the Tudor dynasty, yet during the seventy years of this era there was a subtle shift as a result of Renaissance thought and religious changes known as the Reformation. These changes would impact on certain matters sexual such as the days when a married couple could enjoy sex or the virginity demanded of nuns because they were brides of Christ. Once monasteries were dissolved during the 1530s and 40s, becoming a nun was no longer a possible vocation for a woman. Nuns were turned out of convents and abbeys. The more fortunate of them were granted a pension and returned to their families. Many novices subsequently married.

At the beginning of this period attitudes to sex and sexuality were dictated by the influence of the Roman Catholic Church. The Church has always played a major role in matters of sex. It dictated attitudes and rules that had existed throughout the medieval period and continued into the Early Modern Period. For example, both the adoration of the Virgin and the Fall of Eve helped develop people's views on intercourse, birth, and the function of the human body regarding sex. Women were seen as inferior versions of men. Their sexual organs were even thought to be the reverse of those men possessed. Women were considered susceptible to the devil and dark forces. It was also believed and promoted by the Catholic Church that women's bodies ran cold whilst the male body was inherently hot. They believed that women chased men to acquire heat, sapping their energy in the act of coitus and the release of sperm. Women desired the act of fortification to strengthen themselves so as to dry up bad and superfluous humours which were thought to exist within them.

According to The Tortula, a medieval Compendium of Women's medicine written during the twelfth century in Salerno:

God creator of the universe differentiated the individual nature of things, each according to its kind [...] And wishing to sustain its generation in perpetuity, He created the male and female with provident, dispensing deliberation, laying out in the separate sexes the foundation for the propagation of off spring [...] he endowed their complexions with a certain pleasing commixtion, constituting the nature of the male hot and dry. But lest the male overflow with either one of these qualities, He wished by the opposing frigidity and humidity of the woman to rein him in from too much excess, so that the stronger qualities that is the heat and dryness, should rule the man, who is the stronger and more worthy person [...] and God did this so that the man by his stronger quality might pour out his duty in the woman just as his seed is sown in its designated field and so that the woman by her weaker quality, as if made subject to the function of the man, might receive the seed poured forth in the lap of nature.

Menses was also believed to temper a woman's poverty of heat. It was a way for women to lose excess humours if their periods were regular. Balanced humours were important for health. Male sperm was thought to be hot because they thought it was of the same nature as air. Once received by a woman it could warm her entire body. Therefore, the only way to control women's desires was through marriage and through sex within marriage.

The Church owned a duality of attitude. On the one hand, women were depicted negatively as allegorical images in paintings or on tapestries as vain creatures and temptresses. On the other hand, women possessed the warmth of Mary the Madonna and mother. The temptress Eve was balanced by the importance of the Virgin. A cult of the Virgin had arrived from Byzantium during the medieval period when many shrines and chantries dedicated to Mary the Virgin were constructed and remained revered during the early Tudor period. Henry VII and his son Henry VIII both gave thanks at the Virgin's shrine at Walsingham for the birth of their children.

The admiration of *the Lady* in general was influenced by admiration for the Virgin as the mother of Christ, and was evident in the secular concept of courtly love which had evolved during the thirteenth and fourteenth centuries. This idea concerned ideal love for a lady other than a knight's own wife. The lady, too, could admire a knight but their ideal love was never meant to be physically consummated. It firmly remained part of the fabric of knightly behaviour, poetry and song. Courtly love enjoyed a revival at Henry VIII's court. *Look but touch not the Lady.* Courtly love may even have contributed to Queen Anne Boleyn's undoing since she played the game of love too well.

Since the Church dictated the days on which husbands and wives must not indulge in sex, there was to be no sexual intercourse during Lent,

Advent, on fast days, during Easter week, on Sundays, Wednesdays or Saturdays. The Church decreed there should be no sexual relations while a woman is menstruating, pregnant or during the forty day period after giving birth. Sex was not permitted while a woman was breastfeeding her child. Naturally, many people ignored the Church and followed their own desires. The Church believed that sexual relations were to procreate and were not for pleasure. Therein lies hypocrisy since sex outside marriage was acceptable for men who could take mistresses: in fact, they were often encouraged to do so. The Church turned a blind eye when a husband sought sex elsewhere because abstinence was considered bad for a man's health, and, after all, he could not indulge with his wife during her pregnancy.

The Tudor period marks the transition from the Middle Ages to the Early Modern Era. Renaissance thought, which had evolved in Italy a hundred years earlier, arrived in England during the 1520s. The Renaissance marks a break with the past but at the same time it was an extension of the medieval era. Humanism, the concept of *Roman Humanitas*, brought with it a rediscovery of Classical Greek Philosophy advocating 'Man is the Measure of All Things'. This concept was manifest in art, architecture, politics, science and literature. Renaissance thought encompassed the flowering of Latin and a resurgence of learning based on Classical sources. It heralded a cultural advance. Tudor thinkers such as Thomas More ensured, for example, that their daughters were educated. The consorts of Henry VIII and his two daughters were also highly educated. In time, during the Tudor period, this notion filtered through to the daughters of wealthy merchant gentlemen. Secular female education may have initially been the prerogative of the educated and wealthy fathers but slowly, snail-like, education began to impact generally on wider attitudes towards women's education.

Renaissance students did not reject Christianity. In fact, some Renaissance works were devoted to Christianity. A fascination and study of original Greek scriptures, for example, would lay the groundwork for a Protestant Reformation. Scholars wanted to read scripture for themselves in Greek or Latin and discuss them, not relying on churchmen alone to relay scripture. This, along with advances in printing, enabled texts to appear in the vernacular. If scripture could be read in English and understood in English based on original Greek scriptures rather than the ancient Latin Vulgate, notions regarding the sanctity of the Virgin would come to be questioned. Even so, the temptress Eve still remained the mother of sin for a very long time to come. One aspect of Renaissance thought was concerned with how citizens should behave in public life and present themselves morally. Humanists believed it was important to go into the afterlife with a perfect mind and body attained through education. For them older classical learning and the Bible provided a moral instruction.

The Renaissance revival of learning which came to England during the Tudor era influenced English architecture, music and literature. During the 1520s and 30s King Henry VIII developed palaces in Renaissance style. Large show houses belonging to courtiers and using glass lavishly became a must have. Gardens, too, developed as places for courtiers to play, secreted behind walls and box hedges that were shaped into fantastical animals. Indoor privacy evolved and as well as larger public halls there were many private spaces such as bedrooms and parlours in wealthy homes. A very good example of this kind of building development can be found in the plans of Austin Friars, the London house owned by Thomas Cromwell where servants slept in attic rooms away from family and guests rather than in the hall, kitchens or in corridors. It now became more possible for romantic liaisons to take place in privacy and in secret, although in the eavesdropping, whispering Tudor society nothing remained a secret for long.

The Renaissance occurred during a period when the Catholic Church was dogged by accusations of corruption. Popes were accused of nepotism as never before, guilty of fathering children whom they married into wealthy families to increase their own power. When, in 1517, Martin Luther published ninety-five critical theses challenging Papal authority the Reformation led to a break with the Catholic Church. For centuries the Church had reigned supreme in Western Europe. A new self-awareness evolved in England during the Tudor period as the Church bounced between Catholicism and Protestantism, and, as far as sex and sexuality were concerned, it could be argued that in a quest for the more morally aware man some social conventions became stricter and more priggish than during the medieval period when rules regarding sex and sexuality were often bent or ignored.

*   *   *

As you read this book about matters sexual in Tudor England please be aware of the mores and trends of the period, and the religious and secular beliefs that influenced them. And remember that the past may be a foreign country where 'they do things differently', but also that human emotions endure. In *Sex and Sexuality in Tudor England* we explore how the Tudors viewed birth control, marriage rituals, birth rituals; we consider views on sex existing within and outside the marriage bed; how the Tudors viewed sexual diversity; life in the brothels which harboured Winchester Geese (prostitutes); how they dealt with sexual diseases; how they dressed to kill and danced and strutted to attract; interesting forbidden romantic liaisons; the flowering of romantic Renaissance literature and art; how ordinary people conducted sexual relations; and scandals at court (not all of which ended quite as disastrously as the unfortunate, very sad tragic story of Katherine Howard which opened this introduction).

So take a deep breath and read on. Inhabit the intimate moments enjoyed by the Tudors and enjoy the time-slip listening at their keyholes and peeping into their bedrooms.

# Chapter 1

# The Church, the Lady and Sexuality

S ex has been an integral part of every generation's life. What one might read today in *Hello* magazine would have been no stranger to Tudor Society. There may have been penalties and destroyed lives but love happened regardless, despite it being a time of arranged marriage and often because of it. Love and sex took place between men and women and it occurred between men and between women, despite Church rules that were often ignored.

Any reading of Shakespeare will prove the enduring nature of romantic love and sexual innuendo during the sixteenth century:

> She's beautiful, and
> therefore to be woo'd;
> She is a woman
> Therefore to be won.
> *Earl of Suffolk, Henry VI, Part 1*
> And what about these lines spoken by Balthasar from *Much Ado About
>   Nothing*?
> Sigh no more, ladies,
> Sigh no more
> Men were deceivers ever,
> One foot in sea and
> One on shore
> To one thing constant never.

Chivalry in the early Tudor court had a strong presence even though we tend to associate it more with the High Medieval Period of the twelfth to fourteenth centuries. Yet it was evident during the early Tudor era because it was tied up with the very foundations of the Tudor Dynasty. Henry VII wanted to establish legitimacy and cement his newly won monarchical power to create a legacy that emphasised the conceptual ideals of courtly love and chivalry. He even named his first son Arthur, reminding his subjects of the famous King Arthur, the chivalric king of legend, and, of course, his knights. Notions of courtly love and chivalry would form a framework for courtly conversation and behaviour in Henry's new Tudor court.[1]

Chivalric conduct was recognised as representative of soldierly, manly and courtly behaviour. They were ideals important to the perception of female and male roles in the aristocracy, the military classes and, by Tudor times, ideals often held by the rising middle classes. Tudors took from medieval chivalric code the entire notion of 'an honourable and virtuous person,' a model aspired to throughout many areas of Tudor society. It involved the pursuit of an example of behaviour that actually was impossible to realise. This exemplar influenced the development of chivalric practice in courtly conversation, in literature and in wider society.

Tudor aristocrats enjoyed retelling romantic stories that recalled chivalric victories and which encouraged the model of chivalry and courtly love for men and for women. These were tales of castles, beautiful women and tournaments, held by the two Tudor King Henrys, where ladies selected a knight and offered him a favour to wear in the tournament, just as had happened previously at medieval courts.

Henry VIII, often considered a Tudor Renaissance prince, possessed many chivalric characteristics. He was expert in chasing honour, romance and seeking fame. In his youth Henry enjoyed shared ideals of manhood with other men in tournaments, men such as Charles Brandon who was handsome, manly and married to Henry's sister, Mary. More about them later. The point is that being a man in upper- and middle-class Tudor society meant being elegant, visible and, importantly, accepted within the community. And it was not just for courtiers, but also for men present in the guild hall or presiding over the manor court. Being masculine was to be knightly as well as being engaged with society. The dynamics between gender roles, and especially women's social relationships with men, were so intertwined with the concept of honour that insulting them or offending their honour carried harsh consequences, as we shall see in another chapter. Men competed in the courtship arena to win the affections of a particular woman. Favours might be granted or stolen.

One delightful story tells how Sir Thomas Wyatt, the poet and courtier at King Henry VIII's court, once stole a favour from Anne Boleyn and displayed it to King Henry during a game of bowls. Sir Thomas made overtures to Anne Boleyn when she came to court from France just before the King began to seriously woo her. Wyatt, 'coming to behold the appearance of this new beauty' amongst them, was taken by her 'witty and graceful speech' even more than her looks. He made his advances. She kept her distance. Wyatt was a married man, albeit unhappily, yet Anne did not turn him away because she had observed 'the general favour and good-will she perceived all men to bear him, which might the [sic] rather occasion others to turn their looks to that which a man of his worth was brought to gaze at her, as indeed there after happened.'[2]

Wyatt's grandson, George, relates how while Anne was chatting with Wyatt, he mischievously snatched a small jewel hanging by a lace out of her pocket and hid it within his doublet. No one knew at the time that the King was, himself, in serious pursuit of Lady Anne. If anything, the incident was viewed by others as a flirtation. The King had already taken a ring from her which he wore on his little finger. A few days later Henry and the knightly Wyatt, as well as the King's friends, including his brother-in-law the Duke of Suffolk and Sir Francis Bryan, were all playing bowls watched by a group of ladies. When King Henry claimed the winning roll of the ball, Wyatt challenged the win.

George Wyatt writes: 'And yet still the king pointing with his finger whereon he ware her ring, replied often it was his and especially to the knight he said, "Wyatt I tell you it is mine," smiling upon him withal.' Wyatt realised what Henry was really saying and allowed the King's win. Yet, after a while had passed Wyatt could not resist a return. His grandson writes: 'The knight replied, "and if it may like your Majestie to give it to me to measure it, I hope it will be mine." And withal took from his neck the lace wherat hung the tablet, and therewith stooped to measure the cast, which the king espying knew, and had seen her wear, and therewithal sporn'd away the bowl, and said, " It may be so , but then I am deceived."'

This story is beautifully described in *Graven with Diamonds* by Nicola Shulman, a biography of Thomas Wyatt.[3] The episode illustrates the theme of courtly love prevalent at the Henrician court as a game of love but one that concealed deeper feelings. Wyatt was chivalrous as was King Henry and, of course, Anne Boleyn played the game of courtly love well. Her cousin, Katherine Howard, admitting to physical involvement with Francis Dereham before her marriage to Henry, and to having physical and secret relations with Thomas Culpepper during the royal marriage, simply did not play it as well. Both queens ended up executed. Courtly love, as we shall explore in greater depth later, often carried real and living dangers at King Henry's court.

As Shulman writes, 'We see courtly love acting as a camouflage for real love. Everyone thought the king's ring was "in the ordinary course of dalliance", and that Anne Boleyn is remembered as quite an operator, calculating the value of each courtier's attentions and keeping a strategic silence while she reeled in the king.'[4]

A sinister political slant resulting from Anne's flirtations and the game of courtly love is obvious now, if not at the time, causing alleged affairs to be set up by her enemies in order to bring her down in 1536. Decades after Anne's death Catholic propaganda blamed Anne Boleyn for the advent of The English Reformation. The Catholic Church attacked the reformed Elizabethan Church by questioning Queen Anne Boleyn's personal morals. In response, *The Life of Anne Boleigne* by George Wyatt was circulated at the suggestion of an Elizabethan Archbishop of Canterbury. This book presented a response to Catholic propaganda intent on insulting Elizabeth I's mother, which called Anne 'The Great Whore'. Such propaganda insulted Queen Elizabeth I herself through insidiously questioning the Queen's legitimacy by suggestion.[5]

\*   \*   \*

The early Tudor era was a time of great change, a link between medieval thinking and newer Renaissance ideas, and during this time the Reformation came to England. Did this make for any change to how sexual relations were conducted? The Church tried hard to control people's sexual lives. This had been going on for a very long time, ever since the collapse of The Roman Empire and of its centralised control. In order to fill the gap the Church intervened. Since Christianity preached a moral law backed with threats of hellfire and brimstone, the Church became a 'more effective deterrent than any law-enforcement agency could have devised.'[6]

The Church was present everywhere in every early medieval Western European country, consolidating its power and becoming a major social and religious authority. It drew its notions of morality from the Old

Testament, New Testament as well as the thoughts of early Christian thinkers. Since most people were not literate, the Church's moral grip on villages and towns ran unchallenged throughout the land.

Monastic scholars copied what was considered orthodox and which remained unquestioned for centuries. Church thinking was that sexual sin emerged not from Jesus's own teachings but rather from the considerations of disciples and saints such as St Paul. St Paul set down as early as the first century that celibacy was superior to marriage. He wrote in Corinthians, 'Do you not know that your bodies are members of Christ? Shall I, therefore, take the members of Christ and make them members of a prostitute? Never. Do you not know that he who joins himself to a prostitute becomes one body with her? For it is written the two shall become one flesh.'[7] Worldly obligations would not interfere with devotion to the Lord. Of course, everyone knew this was a conundrum because St Paul also said, 'The husband should give to his wife her conjugal rights, and likewise the wife to her husband.' This sounds confused and inconsistent, and the medieval Church was contradictory. Simply put, St Paul considered that if marriage was good then celibacy was better.

Teachings of St Paul and the important early Christian thinkers such as Tertullian, Jerome, and Augustine left the most lasting impression on Christian sexual beliefs, which mostly continued after the Reformation. After the 1530s the Bible was issued in the vernacular and by Thomas Cromwell's decree a translated Bible was placed in every Church during the mid-thirties when Cromwell held the post of Henry VIII's Vicar-General. Scripture available in translation could now be more easily queried and since more and more Tudors gradually became literate, an individual could ponder scripture for themselves.

Biblical wall paintings in churches, a way for the uneducated to access Biblical stories and hagiography, were whitewashed out during the Reformation, which was in full swing during Edward VI's short reign. Images painted on church walls would have included depictions of Adam and Eve, particularly Eve's partaking of the apple in the Garden of Eden, as well as murals of Heaven and Hell in which devils pulled sinners into Hell's fires to suffer various nasty tortures.

Lust was integral to the doctrine of original sin. St Augustine decreed that man and woman as created by God were initially creatures of the mind, totally in control of their bodies. No excitement could be officially permitted. Naturally, this Church decree was frequently ignored because humans usually enjoy sex and fall in love despite Church views and laws. Sex, as decreed by the Church, was only meant to be for the purpose of reproduction. Adam and Eve fell into lust over which they had no control and every act of coitus performed by humanity after the Biblical fall preached in Genesis was therefore necessarily evil. Every child born of it was born into sin.[8] Only the celibate could ever hope to achieve the perfect state of grace that had been existent before the fall which led to a duality of thinking within the medieval Church.

If enjoying sex was sinful most people were sinners including many clerics. Interestingly, before the eleventh century clerics had married, at least until the latter part of the eleventh century when Pope Gregory VII issued a prohibition on clerical marriage. The Roman Catholic Church viewed marriage as a concession to human moral frailty and it was not until after the Reformation that the clergy were again permitted to marry. As a result, clergy often were driven into secrecy: Archbishop Cranmer had a secret wife, and Cardinal Thomas Wolsey consorted with a mistress and admitted to two illegitimate children, one of whom was called Thomas Winter.

The Catholic Church, as mentioned in the introduction, tried to exercise control when couples had sex. Married couples were supposed to abstain on Thursdays in memory of Christ's arrest, Fridays in memory of his death, Saturdays in honour of the Resurrection, and Mondays in commemoration of the departed. There was a ban on sexual intercourse during fasts and festivals as well as for forty days before Easter, Pentecost and Christmas. Men and women with normal sexual appetites could easily become wracked with guilt because sex in the eyes of the Church was such a great sin. The Church was even officially dictatorial on how sexual relations were physically conducted, considering the 'missionary position' as best for conceiving a male. Other positions could lead to deformity[9] and therefore no sexual experimentation was permitted.

As the act of intercourse was tainted by the fall of Eve, women were considered inferior versions of men. Medical practice at the time was influenced by this concept. Doctors believed that women's bodies ran hot whereas men's bodies ran cold, suggesting that women may have desired the act of fortification. Marriage was, to the Medieval and Tudor mind, the only way to control a woman's desires. So, how young could one marry? The Church decreed the appropriate legal age for marriage as twelve years for a girl and fourteen for a boy. In reality, it was often considered that intercourse should wait until a girl was at least fourteen years old as it could be dangerous for a girl to become pregnant so young. Henry VIII's grandmother, Margaret Beaufort, was married to Edmund Tudor aged twelve. She gave birth to Henry VII before her thirteenth birthday and, as a consequence, the unfortunate Margaret was never able to conceive another child despite two further marriages. She did, however, live to a ripe old age, dying during her grandson Henry VIII's reign. These marriage ages were observed only for the aristocratic classes. Most ordinary Tudor men and women waited until their late teens or early twenties to marry simply because the majority of people could not afford to do so earlier.

Here is another conundrum which is alien to our modern sensibilities. The Church considered sex acceptable for men, so much so that it was permitted for them to take mistresses. Abstinence was considered bad for a man's health so if a man could not have sex with his wife during her pregnancy he could seek it elsewhere and it was not frowned upon by the Church. Henry VIII was famous not only for his six marriages but also for his mistresses. He flaunted Bessie Blount and others, including Mary Boleyn, his mistress of the early 1520s, openly at court. It was not, of course, acceptable for a woman to take a lover. That might place a child's paternity in jeopardy, hence the terribly sad story concerning Katherine Howard referred to in the introduction. In short, an accusation and an admittance of infidelity could have disastrous consequences for a woman.

Did the Reformation of the mid-sixteenth century change Church attitudes towards sex and sexuality in any way?

Christianity was always hostile to sex as pleasure and play. Sex was about procreation. After the Reformation there was an increased emphasis on the woman as a helpmate to her husband, operating as mother and domestic goddess within the middle-class family. Although Protestantism would reject virginity as an absolute ideal, there would be utter condemnation of the unfaithful woman or a woman who entered into sexual relations before marriage. Previously, if the couple was betrothed this was considered as good as marriage. During the 1530s monasteries and nunneries were demolished and sold off. The notion of the virgin nun wed to God disappeared along with these closures. The cult of the Virgin Mary had survived throughout the medieval and early Tudor period as an ideal to believe in and there were many shrines and chantries devoted to her. However, these no longer mattered within the reformed religion.

The Reformation did not bring significant change for couples wishing to divorce. After the Reformation an annulment could only be sought on three grounds: a pre-contract to someone else; consanguinity within the Levitical degrees, which were those relationships defined in the eighteenth chapter of Leviticus; or male impotence of three years, though this was not an easy matter to prove.[10]

If a spouse left home and was not discovered for seven years, the partner could remarry because the assumption was that the missing spouse was dead. However, if he or she returned after a remarriage, the first marriage could take priority over the second, though occasionally the woman might choose the husband she preferred. Divorce was extremely difficult but it was possible, both before and after the Reformation, even though it was frowned upon. Marriage was, for most, a union, breakable only by death.

In Protestant England during the Tudor era sodomy and bestiality became more repugnant than ever. A strong hostility to homosexuality inherited from the medieval Church associated homosexuality with religious heresy. Thomas Cromwell, the king's infamous minister, introduced the Buggery Act in 1533, a law making sodomy illegal for the first time. Prior to this, sexual offences such as buggery were dealt with by the ecclesiastical courts.

During the sixteenth century throughout Europe waves of persecution of homosexuals coincided with the persecution of witches. Both were regarded as dangerous deviants because their existence threatened society's good health. In his book *The Family Sex and Marriage 1500–1800*, Lawrence Stone points out that during the sixteenth century England escaped the worst attacks on sodomy and witchcraft.[11] When Anne Boleyn was put on trial in 1536, one of the accusations against her was that of witchcraft. The King claimed she had bewitched him into his passion for her. It was rumoured at the time that Anne owned a sixth nail which she was in the habit of concealing beneath her flowing sleeve. There were those who considered this blemish a physical sign on her body suggesting guilt of witchcraft. In fact, she was actually accused of 'ill-wishing' the King. Most of the accusations against Anne Boleyn were recorded in later Roman Catholic sources intent on damaging the reputation of her Protestant daughter, Elizabeth I.

During the Tudor era Christianity continued almost completely unchallenged as an explanation of what the universe was and how it operated. Medieval views of Christianity impacted on all aspects of life, including matters sexual. Religious changes were a fiery topic for discussion and so religion became a major focus of conflict. The great upheavals of changing from Catholic to Protestant, back to Catholic and to Protestant again were very confusing for most ordinary people. This was, as Ruth Goodman succinctly puts it in her book *How to be a Tudor*, an issue over which many of England's subjects 'were willing to suffer impoverishment, become social outcasts, or even die.'[12]

To sum up this chapter, at the outset of the Tudor era there had been a 500-year history of celibacy inside monasteries and nunneries throughout the country. During the second decade of the sixteenth century, Martin Luther and others argued that marriage was the proper way for a person to live a holy life, and bringing up children within marriage was a Christian duty and he advocated clerical marriage. Clerics who had secret wives, and Archbishop Cranmer was one such, could declare them, and churchmen could now marry their mistresses. Sex remained at the heart of religious debate, whether it concerned marriage or what was considered as deviant sex, or the age-old profession of prostitution which was stamped upon during the early Tudor era.

# Chapter 2

# Tudor Marriage and Matters Sexual

U nmarried people at this time lived in an in-between world. It simply was more accepted by society to be married and the supposed lack of sexual experience, attributed rightly or wrongly to the unwed, presented amusement to their Tudor peers.[1] Marriage was perceived as essential for the acquisition of respect in society: an unmarried man of fifty was just as embarrassing as an unmarried woman of a similar age. A single man could not take on an apprentice to his trade nor could he stand for public office.

There was interdependence between husband and wife. After all, men needed women to cook, brew, manage the hens, work in the dairy and mind their children. Men ploughed and were in charge of the fields, although if one looks at calendar illustrations from this time women were also working in fields.

Sex was important to the marriage because marriage was importantly for procreation, and without it the marriage was not recognised as a true marriage. The Greeks thought that good sex made the body nimble and light; that it opened pores and purged phlegm. Sex quickened the mind if it was properly enjoyed and drove away melancholy and sorrow. However, they also believed bad sex brought about weakening of mind and body, making man like beasts. Bad sex must have seemed horrific to the high-minded, educated Renaissance man who was well versed in the classics and who aspired to be cultured, sophisticated and, well, civilised. This notion connects with the Greek theory of the four humours which throughout the Tudor era belonged to traditional medical thought. Tudors believed that women were creatures dominated by cold, wet phlegmatic humours with an uncontrollable hunger for sex whereas men could control their appetites. So, during this era most people married and sex within marriage was viewed across society to be a good thing. Never mind St Paul and chastity, that was for monks and nuns, though some clerics and nuns gave way to sin and reportedly broke the rules around chastity.

Sex was not an occupation limited to the bedroom. During the early Tudor era many people lived in communal spaces and those who *did* possess the luxury of their own private bedroom may have had ever-present servants coming and going, or even sleeping in the mistress's bedchamber. Servants undressed and dressed their masters and mistresses as well as fetching and carrying. Early Tudor bedrooms could actually inhibit romantic behaviour within marriage, and don't forget that bedrooms were often shared chambers with children sleeping in the same room as their parents. Of course, this could prove useful. A woman might make the children sleep in the middle of the bed rather than at the sides when she did not want the attentions of her husband.

In Tudor homes you really could not just close the bedroom door and enjoy some privacy. During this period of great Tudor mansions, bedrooms led into other rooms. Homes did not have corridors, as a rule, until the end of the seventeenth century. Fortunately, for cohabiting couples most beds did possess heavy bed curtains, but for those who sought complete privacy lanes and fields might be a more attractive option.[2]

It was universally difficult for a married couple to be private. As for royal children, the whole marriage business was very public indeed. Take, for instance, Henry VIII's sister, Mary Tudor, who was married in 1514 by proxy to the aged King Louis XII of France, a man thirty years older than eighteen-year-old Mary. A proxy bedding following her marriage gave it legality before she set off to France for the actual wedding. Louis could not back out at the last minute and neither could she. After the proxy ceremony poor Mary lay in a bed in 'magnificent dishabille' with her legs bared. Witnesses crowded in, eagerly watching as Louis's ambassador removed his red stockings and took the king's place beside the young bride. Their bare legs moved together and touched. This was the moment everyone rejoiced. Mary was considered legally married. When, on 9 October 1514, she was married with greater ceremony in Abbeville to French Louis, who was thrilled with his beautiful young queen, he said on the following day that he 'had performed miracles' on his wedding night. Louis did not live long after their wedding, and Mary wasted no time. Once it was proved she was not with child, she made a scandalous marriage with Charles Brandon, an English courtier whom she always had loved.

We have already seen that sex was absolutely central to marriage and if there was no consummation the union could be annulled.[3] This situation was used by Henry VIII as one of his reasons for divorcing Anne of Cleves, his fourth wife, in 1540. Henry had married Anne because an alliance with the German State was a good idea for trading and political reasons. Henry, it was reported, was exceptionally disappointed on meeting his new bride. He disliked her appearance and she smelled. She was not elegant or well-read, nor did she understand English dances or play instruments, all talents expected of a Renaissance royal bride. Henry VIII had his chief minister Thomas Cromwell spread the word around court that Henry could not consummate the marriage because Anne lacked physical charms. The King had felt her breasts and belly and found them slack as if she were no virgin. 'I have felt her belly and her breasts, and thereby, as I am able to judge, she should be no maid. Which struck me to the heart ... that I had neither will nor courage to proceed any further.'[4]

This had consequences for Thomas Cromwell. Once he lost favour over the Cleves marriage deal his enemies, which included the Catholic Earl of Norfolk, uncle to Anne Boleyn and Catherine Howard, was able to make the charge of heresy against the Protestant Cromwell stick to him. Cromwell was duly executed on 28 July 1540. Henry married Katheryn Howard on the same day. Anne did well out of the annulment of her marriage to Henry, achieving an excellent settlement, remaining in England, and maintaining a friendship with Henry, led to her being known at court as the 'King's Beloved Sister'.

Sex was a private act but its public function was to create stability in society. It was also a duty to satisfy your partner sexually. In 1557 a book called *The Deceyte of Woman* went to press.[5] This is probably, to the twenty-first century mind, a misogynistic text. It illustrates to its Tudor readership the dangers of sex outside marriage and contains stories of women lying and cheating by taking lovers behind their husband's backs. The suggestion lurking within its pages is that a wife left with no one to fill her bed would find another to do her husband's duty. If it suggests women are morally corrupt, the men who were cuckolded are treated in this book with little sympathy. A man's lack of sexual activity in the marriage bed is perceived as a factor causing his wife to stray.

Another Tudor author writes in an old tale entitled *A Deceit Done in Artois of a Late Time* of a neglected woman's adultery, suggesting that if the woman's husband had remained at home the wife would have not strayed but would have remained happy in her marriage, quite modern in thought for a sixteenth-century text.

Ninety per cent of the adult population reaching adulthood in the sixteenth century married. Some married more than once since marriage defined both social and sexual roles. A father or guardian's obligations shifted because marriage changed a daughter's or son's status. Once wed, men became householders and women became housekeepers. Boys became masters and girls a mistress or dame. A Tudor husband was expected to govern his wife, and in turn his wife was expected to rule those below them. While a man could become a church warden, juryman or reeve, a woman gained status amongst other women. Once she was married she could, for instance, attend a lying in, known as a gossiping, and she could accompany a new mother to her churching. All of these societal inclusions were denied a single woman. Marriage, therefore, provided much sought-after advantages for a woman.[6]

Although the legal age for marriage was twelve for a girl and fourteen for a boy most people married in their mid-twenties. This could be so much younger in the case of the aristocracy, however, because many marriages were designed to further the fortune of family dynasties. Families of relatively similar means or occupations married into similar families because they, the young wife or husband, were expected to bring a fair-share to the marriage. It would, moreover, be very unusual to find a titled man marrying a woman from a common family.[7]

* * *

How did Tudor marriage work? First of all, a marriage union between couples involved a courtship period. Prior to this, prospective parties were engaged in a sequence of enquiries concerning jointures, dowries and relevant property and financial situations. Matchmakers might play a part. These could be friends or relatives or even solicitors. The negotiations were often lengthy since the prospective husband had to demonstrate the ability to support a family. There would need to be agreement between parties, for example, if a dowry would be repossessed by the wife's family should the bride die without a child born to the union.

The courtship period would follow once the settlements were hammered out. It was assumed the courtship time would allow the couple to first develop a friendship and mutual respect rather than love. Love was expected to grow out of friendship. Parents could break off negotiations if it seemed the couple would not be happy. A couple had to both agree to the marriage. Even so, there were situations where a marriage was subtly enforced by parents or guardians, but this enforcement was generally the exception rather than the rule. It may surprise readers but most Tudor parents wanted their children to be relatively happy.

Courtship was controlled and supervised. After all, rumour could threaten a prospective bride's future if a woman ended up pregnant before the formal betrothal, and virtue mattered. Sexual relations counted as consummation, just as a marriage was not a real marriage without it. Courtship though was expected to involve a couple conversing, sharing meals, exchanging gifts, hunting or attending fairs together.

Typical courtship gifts would be coins, ribbons, gloves or similar passed from the man to the woman and signalling the strengthening of their bond. Tokens might carry connotations of sexual and domestic intimacy. Garters might be used as tokens. A bitten root of ginger was another, and, on occasion, rings. An exchange of gifts could also be interpreted as a serious intent of marriage.

Records of matrimonial litigation are held within Church courts from this period, specifically for London, York and Canterbury. They vary and make for fascinating reading as well as an insight into Tudor mores. Some include men motivated by carnal desire involving an exchange of gifts suggesting intent even though the man did not intend marriage. Other litigations concern couples forced to marry following beatings or the threat of death, though marriage was supposed to be consensual. Perhaps the inflated emotions involved cause the court's accounts to seem overly dramatic. The primary focus of the courts was on the precise words said, which required witnesses. The words concerning the giving and accepting of gifts could be used as circumstantial evidence of intention to marry. Let's explore a few cases in brief. The first one refers to a forced union.

In 1487 Robert Rokewode testified how he had discussed dowry and marriage gifts concerning his daughter, Alice, with the prospective groom, a young man called Peter, who contested on the grounds that he only exchanged words of consent under duress. Consent rather than simple affection had to be the legal basis for marriage.

In another case from the same period Robert Allerton testified on his own behalf that 'he often knew a lady named Katherine carnally'. He admitted that they had conceived a daughter, but denied that various tokens were exchanged, rather he had deposited certain gold rings with Katherine for safe keeping. She claimed he also had received gifts from her which were gold rings signifying tokens of love. He denied this fact saying, 'he never had received them from her as from his wife or gave things to her as to his wife, but only the desire of his body satisfying his lust.'[8] He won his case but what happened to poor Katherine and her daughter we do not know.

Courtship was like a dance. The young man's responsibility was to offer gifts and persuade the young bride to agreement. As in a courtly dance of love, a young woman might withhold affection or in turn offer it. Famously, Henry VIII courted Anne Boleyn for seven years while she blew hot and cold, allowing him the odd fondling nature of favour while keeping him distant at the same time. He wrote love letters to her which are to this day archived in the Vatican and which we'll explore later. Henry also famously wrote her poems, also discussed later, and they exchanged gifts. It was a courtship often likened to a hunt. Jane Seymour and Katherine Howard played a similar courtship game in their turn. Contracting marked the end of the courtship.

*  *  *

A formal espousal would prevent poorly worded, poorly witnessed or contested contracts and avoid disputes. Betrothal was a promise to marry which involved a witnessed pledge, using the words 'good will' and 'good liking'. Sometimes during a betrothal ceremony a prayer book was used as well as the services of a priest. The traditional recitation of troths plighted was followed by the joining of hands as in a traditional hand-fasting ceremony. 'I promise to thee that I will be thine husband which I shall confirm by public manner, in pledge whereof I give thee my hand.'[9]

If the couple had not been otherwise precontracted and there was no consanguinity or affinity, there could be no withdrawal from the contract. It was not a simple promise but a legal agreement, and rings were exchanged. A betrothal contract was known as the beginning of the marriage *sponsalia per verba de futuro*. It translates as a promise to marry in the future. This betrothal contract gave rise to no change of status unless it was followed by consummation. It could then be a recognised marriage and was, in fact, recognised as such until the 'Tametsi' decree of the Council of Trent 1545–1563, at least so by the Roman Catholic Church. The Church wanted to save the children of these unions from the stigma of bastardy and parents from the sin of fornication.

Families often celebrated espousals with great festivity. Miles Coverdale, the ecclesiastical reformist, Bible translator and preacher once said, 'In some places there is such a manner, well worthy to be rebuked, that at the hand-fasting there is made a great feast and superfluous banquet…and the couple then esteem themselves as spouse though yet it is not done in Church nor in the street.'[10]

After the betrothal ceremony some couples behaved as husband and wife. Whilst moralists were consistently hostile to sexual intercourse in advance of marriage, thirty percent of brides had children within eight months of marriage. For the most part, the low illegitimate birth rate occurred as the result of broken betrothals.[11]

The code of honour valued chastity and reputation. Virginity remained prized until marriage was secured and imminent. Social and religious pressures made marriage incomplete until it was solemnised in church.

Although hand-fasting declined in popularity during Tudor times, it remained a legal form of marriage as long as there were witnesses. In the north of England hand-fasting was conducted with solemnity and the holding and releasing of hands, with plighting of oaths, kissing, drinking and the ritual exchange of rings before witnesses. The reason for witnesses was obviously that they could prove the marriage had taken place. Nowadays a couple will have a marriage certificate as proof. In Tudor England this was not the case and not until the Council of Trent decreed a marriage void unless performed before a priest and witnesses was hand-fasted marriage problematic. This decree only covered Catholic countries and it was not until 1753 that a similar law, The Marriage Act, occurred in England. A couple could become man and wife by promising themselves to each other, and on occasion, even if witnesses were not present.[12]

Marriages made this way were valid as long as both partners agreed promises had been exchanged. There were those who later wanted to deny the marriage ever took place thus witnesses were important if not necessary. There are records surviving of court cases with witnesses ranging from those who were fellow agricultural labourers to apprentices who shared the couple's lodgings.[13] During the early Tudor period a priest did not have to be present at a clandestine marriage. For example, in 1521 a Buckinghamshire man spoke the following words that made his marriage legal. 'I Robert take thee Agnes to my weddid wife for better for worse and thereto I plight my traught.'[14] Vows could be made before parents or an apprentice's master or even before a group of friends.

Consummation made a marriage legal but wise couples waited until the marriage was secure. Famously, Anne Boleyn made her royal suitor wait years to take her virginity, obviously for various reasons. Even so, she was pregnant when she was officially married to Henry on 25 January 1533 and heavily pregnant when crowned Queen of England on 1 June. It is thought she secretly married Henry during their visit to France in November 1532. She gave birth to Elizabeth on 7 September 1533, importantly born within wedlock, nine months following this visit.

There were issues. Early in 1523 Anne was secretly betrothed to Henry Percy, son of Henry Percy, 5th Earl of Northumberland. This was a love match and the Earl of Northumberland, Henry Percy's father, refused to accept the betrothal. It was broken off. When Cardinal Wolsey refused the match in 1524 Anne was sent home to Hever Castle. Following her departure from court, Henry VIII began his infamous pursuit of Anne, writing her love letters and sending her tokens.

*   *   *

Weddings usually followed a month after the betrothal. The priest called banns three times to ensure there was no reason why the couple could not marry. A bride would be dressed in her best clothes, not necessarily white and often crimson or green. White only became popular for wedding gowns during the nineteenth century. The following description of a Tudor wedding is based on a novel written by Thomas Deloney called *The Pleasant Historie of Jack Newbery*.[15] Written during the late sixteenth century, it tells of Jack's second wedding during Henry VIII's reign. He says that the bride was led to the church between two young boys who had bride-laces and rosemary tied on their silken sleeves. A bride-cup of silver and gilt hung with colourful silk ribbons was carried before her holding a posy of rosemary. Musicians led the procession. Maidens followed carrying bride cakes. Other maidens carried garlands of wheat.[16]

Throughout the sixteenth century the wedding ceremony changed in detail.[17] In the Reformed Church the marriage was performed inside the church, whatever the social degree of the couple. During the early Tudor era most marriages took place at the church door. Only high status weddings were held inside. Whilst a knight married within the door, an earl's child might marry at the choir door. The dowry was announced in public at the church door and the couple were asked if they were willing to be married. Later, the groom laid the ring with an offering of money on a book or in a dish. The priest blessed it, sprinkled it with holy water and placed it on the bride's finger.

Gifts were given to wedding guests. They often were gloves and ribbons. Wedding presents such as plate or jewellery were presented to the couple, usually cast into a basin on a table within the church.[18] For poorer weddings bride ales (festivals) became commonplace. These were held prior to the wedding to raise money for the cost of the wedding through the sale of food and drink.

A wedding had to be consummated for the marriage to be legal and this was the reason for a ceremonial bedding ceremony after the wedding feast. For ordinary people the event could become extremely boisterous. The wedding party played games as the couple were put to bed. Bridesmen traditionally would pull off the bride's garters and fasten them to their hats. Garters were removed from the bride and thrown in the same way a bridal bouquet might be tossed today. The maids would carry the bride to her bedchamber. The bride's undressing, too, was a semi-social rite.[19] After all, it was sex that made it a proper marriage.

A priest traditionally blessed the bridal chamber and bed. Little is actually known about this final scene in the marriage rite other than from literary texts or the bedding ceremony of great people. *Le Fresne* by Marie de France describes the heroine preparing the bedchamber where the priest would bless the newly-weds. Marie de France writes, 'For this was part of his [the priest's] duty.'[20]

*    *    *

Was the bride a virgin? Great importance was attached to the bride's virginal status although the marriage may have already been consummated during the betrothal stage. Other exceptions were a second marriage. How did they know she was a virgin? After the marriage night, throughout the medieval period and early Tudor era, value was attached to the 'bloodied sheet test'. This test has been documented in the Bible, and was written into medieval romances that were widely read in the Tudor era. The sheet was put on display after the wedding night in some noble households as proof of a bride's virginity.

So was Catherine of Aragon able to produce a bloodied sheet after her wedding night with Henry VIII? Apparently, according to one or two sources, she was.[21] I do wonder, however. The bloodied sheet was sometimes a flawed test because there were ways of faking it. The ruptured hymen at first intercourse is not necessarily an accurate test of a bride's virginity. The blood produced may not be from a ruptured hymen. The Greek physician, Sarcanus, suggested any post-coital bleeding was the result of burst blood vessels and denied the presence of any membrane such as a hymen in the vagina. Michael Savonavola, an Italian physician, first used the word hymen in 1498, describing it as 'a membrane broken at the time of deflowering so blood flows,'[22] and references to the hymen as connected to virginity thereafter became commonplace.

In 1573 Amboise Paré, 1510–1590, later claimed there was no such thing as a hymen. Besides, hymens vary in shape and size and thickness, and some bleed while others do not. No matter the value placed on the 'bloodied sheet' test it was no proof of virginity on a wedding night. Henry VIII may have been four times deceived and Catherine of Aragon may not have been a virgin on her marriage night. Anne Boleyn had a history of admirers including a suspected unofficial betrothal to Henry Percy. Katheryn Howard was, by her own admission, no virgin on her wedding night. Katheryn Howard and Francis Dereham allegedly became lovers when she was in the care of her step-grandmother, Agnes Howard, Dowager Duchess of Norfolk, addressing each other as 'husband' and 'wife'.

Medieval virginity tests were urine focused. These may have been used during the early Tudor period in some instances. The Italian physician, Niccolo Falcucci, suggests:

If a woman is covered with a piece of cloth and fumigated with best coal, if she is a virgin she does not perceive its odour through her mouth and nose; if she smells it, she is not a virgin. If she takes a drink, she immediately voids urine if she is not a virgin. A corrupt woman will also urinate immediately if a fumigation is prepared with cockle. Upon fumigation with dock flowers, if she is a virgin she immediately becomes pale, and, if not, her humor falls on the fire and other things are said about her.[23]

There was also the sparkling urine test,[24] which hails from the thirteenth century. It was suggested in Albertus Magnus's *De Secretis Mulierum* that the urine of virgins is 'clear and lucid, sometimes white, sometimes sparkling.' There may have been many dwelling in remote Tudor villages who believed in this utter nonsense.

Medical texts of the period referred to methods that might prove virginity. There were, equally, methods to restore the semblance of virginity according to some medical references. *The Trotula* is a medieval Compendium of Woman's Medicine. It has advice on how a girl can fake it.[25] This suggests a way for the vagina to appear unpenetrated so these brides would appear as virgins: 'Let her take ground sugar, the whites of eggs, mix them in rainwater in which pennyroyal and herbs of this kind have been cooked, and with a new linen cloth dipped in this place it in the vagina two or three times a day. And if she urinates at night, put it in again. And note that prior to this the vagina ought to be washed well with the same water with which these things are mixed.'[26]

Another suggestion is: 'Take the newly grown bark of a holm oak. Having ground it, dissolve it in rainwater, and with a linen or cotton cloth place it in the vagina in the above-mentioned manner. And remove all these things before the hour of the commencement of intercourse.'[27]

According to Canon law a woman's virginity might be inspected by women of good repute. The idea goes back to the examination of the Virgin after the birth of Christ by the midwife Salome. Based on an *apocryphal gospel*, it was occasionally acted out in medieval drama scenes of the nativity.[28]

Bear in mind how the Church looked on marriage as necessary for procreation. Impotence, if it could be proved, was a ground for annulment and divorce. Even so, it was almost impossible to bring a successful case regarding impotence in the Church courts. Besides, neither partner was free to remarry while the other lived, even if the divorce was granted. Impotence was also a lawful impediment to marriage if kept secret from the bride, and, perhaps embarrassingly, was one of those lawful impediments that could be announced at the church door. If an annulment for this reason was granted, both partners could remarry. 'No sex, no children, no point!'[29]

The Church did not trust women to be truthful. Once wed, the couple had to be married for three years before such a case could be brought to court. If the husband denied the accusation, witnesses would have to be produced to testify the wife was a truthful sort of person and of good character. It was the same if the husband admitted impotency. Since the Church court demanded proof, it was not unusual for a group of trusted matrons, a priest and a congress to be consulted. The matrons would subject the accused man to a bedroom trial and would make efforts to elicit an erection.[30] Poor man – it must have been a hideous experience. The report below is one example of this embarrassing occurrence: 'The ... witness exposed her naked breasts and with her hands warmed at the said fire, she held and rubbed the penis and testicles of the said John. And she embraced and kissed the said John, and stirred him up in so far as she could show his virility and potency, admonishing him for shame that he should then and there prove and render himself a man. And she says, examined and diligently questioned, that ... remaining without any increase or decrease.'[31] The report continues, 'Whereupon with one voice the assembled women cursed John for not being "better able to serve and please" his wife and left court.'[32]

Couples across the social spectrum used Church courts to solve their matrimonial problems. They took advantage of the Church's teaching on marriage. Before the Reformation the bishop possessed the power to judge for his church, but generally most cases were handled by judges appointed by the bishop. The defender of the bond was a canon lawyer whose job was to represent the diocese acting as a watchdog over the diocese. He would have notaries to swear in witnesses. After the Reformation the ecclesiastical courts held the authority of the Crown because Henry VIII made himself Defender of the Faith and Head of the Church rather than the Pope. It was all to an end rather than entirely for a true religious reason. Henry VIII was not Protestant and after his break with Rome continued to burn heretics for not accepting the Catholic notion of transubstantiation. In 1533 Henry VIII, now Head of the Church, demanded the Archbishop of Canterbury grant him a divorce from Catherine of Aragon.

Nothing significant changed with the advent of Protestantism. Sex between married couples was strictly encouraged by Puritans emerging later in the Tudor era. Puritans did not object to sex within marriage, just outside it. 'How should their matrimony bee otherwise a means of preventing whoredom? ... How should it be a comfort in their lives? How a furtherance to their better glorifying of God.'[33]

Procreation remained the most important purpose for marriage. However, since women were becoming more generally literate subtle change would eventually bring about changes in their condition as wives and mothers. The cases mentioned above were rarer after the Reformation. Marriage, despite the ability of King Henry VIII to achieve divorce twice, and the fact that clergymen could marry after the English Reformation, remained for life. Divorce was frowned upon and incredibly difficult to achieve in Protestant England.

## The Bedding Ceremony

For most Tudors life did not begin with conception. It began when a man's seed entered 'the woman's privitie', as the neck of the womb is referred to by at least one physician. Male seed was met by a matching seed, released by the woman during sex. Tudors considered this the basic recipe for creating a child. Most hoped for boys and believed boy foetuses occupied the right chamber of a subdivided womb whilst a girl occupied the left. It is, of course, yet another medieval myth. Medievals and Tudors deemed actual new life to begin when the soul entered a fully-formed foetus at forty-six days for a boy and ninety days for a girl before he or she was considered a person.[1]

Further myths existed around determining the sex of a child. A large number of people believed that those anxious for a boy should refrain from sexual intercourse when the wind blew southwards since this would likely result in a girl. If a Tudor woman scrutinised her reflection she could tell if the foetus could be a boy. If carrying a girl, the mother would have a heavy and swarthy appearance and melancholic eye. Boys apparently lay higher in the womb than girls due to their heat. A girl would be at the bottom of the womb because of her coldness and weight. Carrying a girl could affect a woman's health more adversely than carrying a boy.[2]

*   *   *

The sex of the child was of particular importance for one late medieval marriage: that of Elizabeth of York and Henry VII. Their marriage followed a decades' long civil war between the Houses of York and Lancaster. The Lancastrian heir, Henry VII, had won his crown from Yorkist Richard III at Bosworth and his subsequent marriage to Elizabeth of York helped to consolidate his kingly position by uniting the warring Houses. It created a new dynasty of Welsh Tudors. At the time, one foreign ambassador wrote, 'everyone considers [the marriage] advantageous to the kingdom.'[3]

When Henry VII married Elizabeth of York the burden was on her to produce male heirs quickly. Shortly after arriving in London, Henry placed her in his mother, Margaret Beaufort's household at Coldharbour, a medieval manor house close to London Bridge, and one of a series of houses Henry VII would renovate in the current, fashionable Burgundian style. He made sure it had glazing, possessed shiny cupolas and had richly furnished galleries and chambers.[4]

Theirs was not a love match as Elizabeth's parents, Edward IV and Elizabeth Woodville, had previously enjoyed. The country changing hands between Yorkist and Lancastrian claimants during The Wars of the Roses meant that Lancastrian Henry Tudor desperately needed Yorkist Elizabeth to legitimise his kingship. By December 1485 Parliament had approved their union. Princess Elizabeth of York would be Queen of England. The pair were related in the fourth and fifth degree of kinship and thus required papal dispensation. It was speedily secured in December 1485 and the wedding hurriedly took place at Westminster Abbey on 18 January 1486.

It cannot have been an easy for this princess. She had experienced a sheltered girlhood and an exceptionally uneasy one. Her mother's family were extremely unpopular. Elizabeth's young brothers had been placed in the Tower by her uncle who took the throne as Richard III and after this the little boys were never seen again. Elizabeth's male relatives were executed, and to add insult to injury Richard III proclaimed Elizabeth illegitimate, giving rise to reports that her father and mother's marriage was invalid because her father Edward IV had been betrothed previously to another woman. Despite all this, Elizabeth had the best Yorkist claim to the throne.[5]

Did Henry bed Elizabeth before their wedding ceremony? If he did have sex with his betrothed before the event it would have been after Parliament's go-ahead for their marriage, or maybe because he wanted to ensure she was fertile. If he died without an heir the Tudor dynasty would be extremely short-lived. A verbal promise of marriage was perceived by Tudors and Medievals as a binding agreement. Henry may, indeed, have bedded her at his mother's Cold Harbour house prior to their wedding to make her feel more at ease before the bedding ceremony which could be a daunting experience. Whatever the reason, Henry's bride was fertile and their first child, Prince Arthur, was born eight months later.[6]

Elizabeth was tall, pretty and blond, in possession of typical pink and white Plantagenet beauty and defined by chroniclers as having long, flowing golden locks and even features. Her parents, Edward IV and Elizabeth Woodville, were notoriously good-looking. Henry Tudor, at ten years her senior, had pale blue watchful eyes and dark hair curled in European fashion. As the progenitor of a powerful new dynasty he was perceived as wise and prudent. A rapid production of heirs would confirm his claim to England's throne.

Elizabeth of York would have worn rich clothes and jewellery to her wedding but not white, which was not usually worn for Tudor weddings. She probably chose velvet in a rich tawny blue, purple or crimson. We do not have an actual record of her outfit. Embroiderers and seamstresses, furriers and jewellers would all have worked hard on the gown which must have been exceptionally sumptuous in order to send out the message that this wedding was the beginning of the Tudor dynasty. The gown would have been embellished with gold gilt threads and set with intricate lace, delicate filigree tissue and silk ribbons. Ornamentation was important to advertise status so the more embellishment the better. She would have worn her golden hair loose or caught up in a net scattered with pearls and golden tassels. Henry is known to have loved ermine and wore purple gold of cloth tissue and a shirt of crimson silk. His doublet was satin. His shirt was laced with ribbons. A cap of crimson, decorated with gold, and a surcoat trimmed with ermine, along with a velvet belt completed his ensemble.[7]

They were married by the Archbishop of Canterbury. The wedding ring was a solid gold band that weighed two-thirds of an ounce. This was to be worn on the ring finger of the left hand. Tudors believed the ring, once blessed by the priest or in this case the archbishop, would protect against unkindness and discord. After the nuptials they arrived at Westminster Hall where they retired to a private chamber before the wedding feast. One wonders if the royal cooks prepared any foods known to excite lust: chestnuts, pistachios and pine nuts were used in folk medicine to stimulate libido while meat could strengthen a husband's potency and aid a wife's fertility.[8] A subtlety would be served between courses. This was a fancy sculpture of marzipan and spun sugar. The most loved design for posh weddings was a model of the new wife shown in later stages of pregnancy. Tudors were not prudish about phallic-shaped foods such as asparagus and those that might suggest bawdy jokes such as the newly discovered 'apricock'.

As with all royal weddings, there was protocol on seating and service. Tables set with damask cloths were scattered with flowers and herbs and best cutlery and plates. The nef, the ship-shaped vessel with salt or spices, was placed in front of the bride and groom and marked their high status. Carvers, sewers, cupbearers, pantlers with bread, ewers, and waiters were choreographed by the Master of the Hall who announced guests' arrival.

The wedding feast and pageantry led to the bedding ceremony, the event almost as important as the wedding ceremony, if not more so. The bedding ceremony for a medieval and Tudor couple was made deliberately public. For a royal couple sexual failure could have drastic dynastic consequences. It was therefore important that members of the court and household were given sufficient reassurance that the act had been satisfactorily performed on the wedding night.[9] Everyone hoped and prayed that an heir would follow the wedding night with speed. 'From their two bodies one heir might succeed,' wrote the chronicler Edward Hall. This would challenge any upstart Yorkist rivals claiming the throne.[10]

There were rules for a royal bedding ceremony. At around 8pm Elizabeth's ladies escorted her to the bed chamber. Most likely, Elizabeth and Henry passed their first married night in The Painted Chamber at Westminster, which was certainly spacious and luxurious. Henry III had commissioned a mural for it depicting the coronation of Edward the Confessor and, moreover, it was heated by a huge fireplace, necessary as this was a midwinter event. The chamber even contained a private chapel. It had a view of the river and pleasantly overlooked a series of narrow gardens. Henry VII's bed was grand and ornate, dominating the chamber at apparently sixteen spans broad and fourteen long. It had tall bed posts, unlike earlier beds. In fact, the grand four-poster bed was a Tudor innovation. A canopy and curtains protected the couple from vermin that could drop on them during the night. Thick woollen curtains kept out draughts and noise. Since Elizabeth and Henry married in the middle of winter the royal bed would have been made up with layers. There was the bedstead, feathered bolster, a fustian, a woollen cloth, a bottom sheet, pillows, the top sheet, and quilts of scarlet, a high quality wool cloth from the Netherlands valued for its colour and softness. They would also have a damask counterpane. As Henry favoured ermine covers these may have provided extra warmth.[11]

The bedding ritual commenced in this luxurious setting. Elizabeth was undressed and put to bed. Henry, meanwhile, stripped down to his shirt which would have reached mid-thigh. Accompanied by his gentlemen attendants, musicians, priests and bishops, handsome Henry joined Elizabeth in the great bed. Clerics would murmur blessings over them with a sprinkling of holy water. Wine and spices were served, including sharp spices such as pepper, cinnamon and cloves to sweeten their breath, engender strength, give the pair courage and benefit their digestion after the wedding feast. Onlookers may have lingered to catch a glimpse of their legs touching or the royal couple kissing or even embracing. After the courtiers finally bade the pair goodnight and departed Elizabeth and Henry enjoyed some privacy.

However, one wonders if they were truly private. It was usual for royalty to be attended during the night or at least have servants positioned outside the bedchamber door. As Tracy Borman points out in *The Private Lives of the Tudors*, it was little wonder servants played a key role in the exposure of adultery or the dissolution of an unsuccessful marriage. A thick curtain drawn around the bed did at least prevent a couple being overlooked. The morning after a significant bedding ceremony the bloodstained bed sheet was displayed to the whole household, though perhaps not on this occasion.[12]

On the morning following the wedding night Henry presented Elizabeth with a 'morning gift', which, we are told, was a poem by Giovanni de Gigli. Afterwards, Elizabeth took part in her uprising ceremony and was dressed for the day. Since Prince Arthur was born on 20 September, eight months after the nuptials, Elizabeth had passed the marriage test. She had proved to be a fertile York princess.[13]

After the wedding night Elizabeth was set up in her own apartments. She had a bedchamber of her own which Henry would visit to indulge in sex with his queen. Such occasions were preceded by a private supper in her apartments. Once Elizabeth was pregnant, Henry would have abstained from conjugal visits. She had paid her marriage debt for now. Also, sex during pregnancy was believed to be detrimental to the health of the child in the womb. At this time it was usual for a king to take a mistress during his wife's pregnancies to keep him virile. If Henry VII had taken mistresses there is no evidence in contemporary sources (unlike his son, Henry VIII).

\*   \*   \*

Another important bedding ceremony would come to dominate a Tudor queen's future married life. Catherine of Aragon arrived in Plymouth in 1501 following a gentle crossing of the southern channel. She married Prince Arthur six weeks after her arrival in England. London streets were decked out with pageants for the wedding and filled with celebratory dance and song as Arthur and Catherine processed from the Tower to Westminster Abbey. On the wedding day Catherine was led into church by ten-year-old Prince Henry. A 6-ft-high platform was set up inside covered with red worsted cloth. Unusually, this couple was dressed in white. A four-course feast and 'costly disguisings' was held in the Bishop's Palace followed by the married couple's bedding ceremony in Bayard's Castle. It was to become the most controversial wedding night in Tudor history.[14]

Friends witnessed Arthur climb into bed and receive the priest's blessing that they would be protected from 'phantasies and illusions of devils'.[15] From this point on only Catherine and Arthur knew what really happened. *Edward Hall's Chronicle*, written in the 1540s, insisted, 'this lusty prince and his beautiful bride were brought and joined together in one bed naked and there did that act which to the performance and full consummation of matrimony was most requisite and expedient.' Hall was only three years old at the time of the royal wedding. By the time he was writing it was accepted in court circles that Arthur and Catherine had sex during their short wedded life.

Servants' testimonies, as well as witnesses, were crucial after Henry VIII challenged the legitimacy of his own marriage to Catherine and requested it dissolved by the Pope. The events of the wedding night in 1501 would be analysed and debated for centuries. Catherine later claimed they shared a bed on seven occasions but there was never full consummation. Her waiting women and Arthur's gentlemen were divided on the issue. It was suggested their sexual passion had weakened Arthur who was already frail.[16] This accusation paralleled another suggestion at the time that Catherine's brother Juan died in 1497 because his allegedly passionate wife, Margaret, had exhausted him.

At one of the 'disguisings', held along with tournaments to celebrate the wedding of Arthur and Catherine, eight 'goodly knights' were hired to overcome the resistance of eight 'goodly and fresh ladies' who yielded to the forces of love. Here there was a romantic subtext, but, sadly, the following March Arthur and Catherine both fell ill at their home in Ludlow to 'the sweat', a flu-like disease. Catherine survived but Arthur died on 2 April. She was a widow after only four months of marriage. It is possible that Arthur also suffered from tuberculosis and this also caused his death.[16] Tracy Borman, in her book *In Bed with the Tudors* says that Catherine's physician, Dr Alcaraz had testified that Arthur had been unable to perform the sexual act: 'The Prince had been denied the strength necessary to know a woman, as if he was a cold piece of stone, because he was in the final stages of phthisis (consumption)'.[17] Arthur had weak limbs and according to this doctor, was exceedingly thin. The doctor claimed he had never seen such thin limbs previously in any young man. Interestingly, if it was testicular tuberculosis that can cause increased libido temporarily but dampen actual performance. If so, this particular disease might explain Arthur's inability for the full consummation of his marriage with Catherine of Aragon. This is a theory and still in the realms of speculation. Of course, historians do not know conclusively if Arthur did or did not consummate the marriage.

# Chapter 3

# Medical Practices and Beliefs Associated with Childbirth and Contraception

Pregnancy was the expected outcome of sexual relations, but childbirth in Tudor times was hazardous. Jane Seymour, Henry VIII's third queen, went into seclusion on 16 September 1537 for her confinement, and, as was the custom, she was attended by midwives and some of her married ladies. No man except the King and her chaplain could now see her before the birth. Traditionally, the room where she would live until she delivered her child was kept extremely warm with only one window uncovered. The birthing chamber's floor was carpeted and candles constantly lit, creating a soft light but also adding to the apartment's already suffocating heat. A pallet lay on the floor beside the expectant mother's bed which was where she would give birth.[1]

Jane's married ladies served her throughout her seclusion. Everything she needed, including her meals, were delivered to her chamber door. At last, some four weeks later, Jane's birthing pangs began. Masses were offered up for her in every parish church throughout London. A solemn procession made its way from St Paul's Cathedral to Westminster Abbey, led by the clergy wearing ceremonial robes and followed by the mayor and aldermen. Merchant guilds and city livery companies also joined the procession and prayed for Jane's safe delivery.

Jane Seymour's labour turned out to be a difficult one. With a girdle containing a prayer of supplication to St Margaret of Antioch placed around her enormous waist, and after hours of labour, she finally gave birth to a long-awaited prince. King Henry was jubilant. Heralds were dispatched to every corner of the kingdom, A *Te Deum* was sung in every parish church in the land and Cathedral bells rang out.

The prince was christened Edward in the new Chapel Royal at Hampton Court on the evening of Sunday, 15 October following a magnificent torc-lit procession led by ushers, squires, knights and household officers.

Bishops, abbots and clergy walked behind them. The four-year-old Lady Elizabeth, carried by Lord Beauchamp, bore Edward's embroidered white baptismal robe and the chrisom oil. The baby prince followed, carried on a cushion held by the Marchioness of Exeter. Sybil Penn, Edward's wet nurse, and the midwife who delivered him were also present. Lady Mary, Henry's elder daughter, was in attendance as Edward's godmother, as well as a great number of the English aristocracy and the King's excited council.

After the baptismal ceremony Jane and Henry received the christened prince and their guests in Jane's apartment. Queen Jane wore crimson velvet lined with ermine and she lay on a rich pallet bed, propped up by cushions of crimson damask and cloth of gold. She blessed her son. Henry, too, blessed the baby and wept for joy. The Duchess of Suffolk returned Edward to his nursery while refreshments were served. On the Christening day, Jane was well.

However, before Edward was many days old this situation changed as Jane suddenly grew extremely ill. After eating a dish of salmon in a white wine sauce with onions and verjuice she suffered gripping pains in her stomach and felt tingling in her hands and feet. She developed shortness of breath as well as an exceptional thirst and a high temperature. As the days wore on the queen suffered shortness of breath and pains in her chest; her ankles were swollen. Eventually the Queen turned blue and struggled for breath. She was dying and received the last sacraments. The fact that she was extremely cold suggests she died a result of postpartum infection. Alison Weir suggests in *Jane Seymour, The Haunted Queen* that there may have been two illnesses; the first being food poisoning and the second dehydration and embolism which led to heart failure. She possibly had also developed a clot in her leg and grown anaemic after her postpartum blood loss.[2]

While Jane Seymour's death remains a mystery to this day, it illustrates the dangers of childbirth and how medicine at this time did not have any answers. Childbirth, the desired result of sex in the eyes of the Church, and, indeed, by most couples, was exceptionally risky in Tudor times. Puerperal fever was very common, but other risks abounded too. Henry VIII's mother, Elizabeth of York, was also a casualty of childbirth. Henry's grandmother, Margaret Beaufort, who gave birth to Henry VII aged only thirteen, was never able to conceive again despite her further marriages. Katharine Parr, Henry's sixth wife, died as a result of childbirth when finally married to Thomas Seymour, Jane's brother. Statistically, one in five Tudor women died from complications either during or after birth.[3]

In general childbirth took place in a closed world where men were unwelcome. The bedchamber for middling sorts of women – those who did not have the luxury afforded the nobility of special chambers set aside for the occasion – would be filled with busy women known as gossips. These could include witnesses, midwife assistants and the midwives themselves. A midwife might arrive with wise women from amongst her neighbours. She would supervise the birth and be involved in the baptism and christening ceremony and would have to be provided with food for the duration of her stay. All this would be expensive for a financially struggling husband who would have to pay the midwife and her attendant nurse.

Midwives were generally respectable upholders of sexual propriety and most were widows or married women. Midwives were the principal support for women in labour, taking temporary control of her household. Other women respected her knowledge and experience. The midwife was in charge of the birthing chamber's light and heat and she would arrange furniture and give out instructions to others. Often the midwife arrived at the birth with a birthing chair. Other paraphernalia would include a knife, sponge, binders and oil of lilies or almonds to anoint the labouring woman's womb and her own hands. She, alone, could touch the labouring woman's genitals. She would remove rings and bracelets and her nails were trimmed, her hands washed. During the birth she would probe, pull, advise and comment on progress as well as employing purges, liniments, poultices, ointments and herbal infusions to help the labouring woman. It was also her task to bathe, lubricate, talk to and comfort the labouring woman during childbirth. She swaddled the newborn and presented her/ him to the waiting father. At normal baptisms she carried the child to the font. Only in cases of severe complications would a male physician intervene and for the ordinary woman, particularly a village woman, a physician was unlikely to even be found to help. A midwife could also administer the sacrament of baptism if a baby seemed likely to die.[4]

Midwives, by the reign of Elizabeth I, were encouraged to have licenses to practise midwifery. A statute of 1512 had made bishops responsible for issuing these to male practitioners. By the mid-century Andrew Bode in his *Breviary of Health* encouraged bishops to extend this to midwives. It was a check on her orthodoxy and good reputation and to remove those midwives who might possess unreformed superstitious practices,[5] though there is no evidence to suggest that midwives were ever involved in witchcraft or that witches were ever midwives.

*    *    *

The early modern period was still dominated by medieval medical practice and beliefs. Joyful birthing scenes we can see depicted on Italian celebratory trays during this era contain idealistic births showing happy female attendants exchanging gifts, playing music and enjoying animated conversation. An inscription on such a tray might state, 'May God give health to every woman who gives birth … May the child be born without fatigue or danger.'[6] It is a genuine sentiment but one that was often at variance with reality. Childbirth so easily could go wrong.

A Shrine Madonna was a sculpture that acted as a tool for individual and communal prayer. The Madonna would act as an altarpiece around which people could gather. In times of crisis a Shrine Madonna could be opened up to reveal an internal panoply of scenes. It was as if the very image of Mary was itself incorporating a world both earthly and heavenly. Hers was, after all, the saintly womb in which Christ had been incubated.[7] Often the Virgin's statue was crafted as an ark containing a precious burden always protected by a doorway. It would be opened up into a triptych on those important and significant occasions when pregnancy was slow in coming or during prayers given up for the safe delivery of a child. On other occasions this Madonna could be prayed to when a couple desired a child and also with thankful prayers after a successful birth. Catherine of Aragon was known to visit the Madonna shrine at Walsingham. Henry VIII visited the Priory of Our Lady of Walsingham to give thanks for a son born to Catherine in 1511. Henry removed his shoes on that occasion and proceeded to walk barefoot to the Virgin's shrine where he lit a candle and offered the shrine a costly necklace as a gift.[8] Sadly, the little prince Henry VIII had with his first wife did not live long.

*    *    *

A long tradition of belief connecting spiritual morality and earthly health existed in Tudor England. People thought religious intervention to be just as effective concerning the cure of illness as the doctrine of four humours which dominated medical thinking at this time (and which will be explained in the next chapter). Jane Seymour wore a prayer belt while giving birth to Edward and the entire city prayed for her safe delivery. Many Tudors believed that good deeds on earth might be traded for instant good health. Before the Reformation pilgrims would leave money, candles, and wax effigies of afflicted body parts at religious shrines hoping for spiritual favour.

While The Virgin Mary may have been thought to have conceived through heavenly means, medical authorities, even during the sixteenth century, knew that the womb was part of a larger sexual system within the female body. Doctors had known about the cervix, vagina, ovaries and the clitoris for centuries. With the advent of the Renaissance and its interest in new learning and investigation of classical texts, there was a little more heed paid to rational thought and Renaissance physicians were curious to discover more.

Renaissance anatomists claimed to have discovered the clitoris. Firstly, Renaldo Colombo (1515–1559) was the chair of anatomy at the University of Pisa. He stated the existence of the 'quimberry' in his book *de re Anatomia* in 1559. Gabriele Falloppio (1523–1562) was famous for the discovery of the fallopian tube and published his discovery in *Observations Anatomicae* in 1561, claiming he wrote the book back in 1550. Doctors had been aware of the clitoris for centuries and women knew where their 'quimberry' was. Falloppio, referring to the clitoris incorrectly, claimed 'It is so hidden that I was the first to discover it.'[9]

The anatomists of the era based their work on the dissection of cadavers. This was not an easy mission since dissection was, throughout the medieval period, disproved by the Catholic Church. Dissection was extremely rare and the first public dissection north of the Alps had occurred back in 1404. The new information regarding sexual anatomy was how the anatomists understood that the clitoris was an organ, not just a pleasure spot to be massaged during sexual activity.

Renaissance thinkers heralded the knowledge that the clitoris was important to sex and pleasure. It was the principle seat of a woman's enjoyment in intercourse and it also caused the woman's seed to 'flow in all directions'. Indeed, people believed that a woman needed to enjoy sex for a baby to be conceived. This is another duality of thought concerning sex at this time.[10] Medieval doctoral students studied Avicenna, one of the most important Persian physicians and writers from the much earlier Islamic Golden Age, who had claimed in the eleventh century that a large clitoris allowed women to perform coitus, similar to that with a man, but with another woman. His *The Canon of Medicine* became a standard medical text used in medieval universities until 1650.[11]

The Greek and Roman world had a highly developed theoretical and practical framework for understanding health[12] and these beliefs were passed to medieval and Tudor thinkers. They believed that nature is composed of four elements—fire, water, air and earth. The four basic elements were linked to moisture and heat and affect the external and internal properties of everything in existence. The basic element fire was hot and dry; water was wet and cold; earth was dry and cold; air was hot and wet. Similarly, the Greeks believed that the human body consisted of four internal components known as humours: blood, phlegm, yellow bile and black bile. They believed a person's constitution was determined by the equilibrium of these substances and that each humour was linked to an element— black bile to earth, yellow bile to fire, blood to air and phlegm was related to water. Misalignment of the humours could plunge someone into ill health or even death.

Hippocrates and his followers believed that mind and body were a single entity. During a disease the mind would have effects on the physical body and vice versa. They also believed that an excess of one of the humours brought about a specific temperament in people and therefore a lack of balance between the humours influenced people's way of acting, feeling and thinking. If one was melancholic one would have an excess of black bile and be sensitive. Choleric people had predominantly yellow bile and were passionate and quick to anger. Sanguine personalities had an excess of blood and were confident, optimistic and sociable. A person who was phlegmatic was a deep thinker, fair, calm, willing to compromise and hard working.

A variety of treatments were available which would be used to correct an imbalance. Purges and tailored prescriptions using fiery roots and spices, cooling herbs and balms might restore a patient to good health. Blood-letting and the use of leeches to draw blood were both used widely to correct the imbalance. Jane Seymour, who probably was anaemic, suffered blood-letting at least once in the days before she died— a serious misdiagnosis. The theory of the humours gets even more complicated as the planets were also thought to affect the human body. With blood-letting, for instance, blood was taken from bodily parts linking the birth star of the patient to the current heavenly position of the appropriate planet or star. Physicians even carried medical charts to provide advice to students and patients on the practice.

The system of four humours was revered, taking precedence over actual bodily observation.[13] Even if a method was questionable, doctors still followed it, as in the case of Jane Seymour. Changes in medical thinking would come slowly and the doctrine of the four humours survived as a popular doctrine far into the eighteenth century.

It becomes even more relevant to sexuality because there was a humoral distinction between the sexes. Women, to remind you, inclined towards cold and dry. Men were deemed warm and moist. The female body was also considered biologically subordinate to that of the male. Their sexual parts were the reverse of a man's; the male turned inside out. Men, unsurprisingly in Tudor times, formed the true ideal for mankind as they produced warmth; they grew larger than women and they possessed more bodily hair than a woman. They disposed humoral excess through the production of sperm and sweat. Women's bodies, on the other hand, were colder, more like those of children, and their growth was slower. Women tended towards physical weakness and fragility. For women menstruation was the method of purging excess.[14] Women were, after all, the weaker sex.

By the dictates of humoural theory menstrual blood could be used to make judgements as to a woman's constitution. A large woman with heavy reddish menses would be most likely prudent and chaste. A heavy flow of bluish blood indicated female inconsistency. Other types of blood might indicate a woman's good memory or inactive mind.[15] Roman Catholic theology even viewed childbirth as a woman's share of punishment for original sin and if a woman suffered, she suffered for this very reason. Unfortunately, Jane Seymour, along with all the other Tudor women who endured horrendous childbirths and never recovered afterwards, could be numbered amongst them.

Churching was a hugely important ceremony for a Tudor woman to undergo after childbirth. For the merchant class, knightly class and nobility the tradition of churching usually happened for a whole month following childbirth, giving the new mother time to rest after her ordeal. Churching was a religious postpartum ceremony required of secluded women prior to their reintegration into society and was variously referred to as 'Purification', 'Thanksgiving' or the 'Churching of Women'.[15] This practice was not generally followed by peasant women who had no time to spare in their busy lives and might even have given birth in the fields during the harvest period. The impoverished mother had to get back to work as soon as possible following a birthing.

Later in the sixteenth century the ritual of Churching became embroiled in the church's contest with Protestantism. Churching after childbirth had social, sexual and festive connotations that lay beyond the Church's scope, and despite some objection, therefore continued. Prior to this ceremony a new mother would attend her church veiled, with her child carried by the midwife or another female. A service of purification with its own litany followed. Churching occupied a special place in the woman's world of the time, a place always associated with fecundity and motherhood. This ceremony was a rite of passage that was connected to female pollution, possibly originally a ritual designed to control women who were considered potentially sinful and even unclean. The actual service focused on 'restoration and cleansing after the impurity and sequestration of childbearing.'[16]

By Tudor times it had morphed into becoming a popular social gathering, for the most part a collective female occasion celebrated by women with women. It might even, as the social aspect evolved, be viewed as resistance to male control, exemplifying a feminist custom of women themselves taking charge. Gossipings, a tradition of married women and widows collecting together, became associated with the very feminine purification ceremony. The day involved conviviality and display, feasting and drinking following the visit to church. This festivity was looked upon as a woman's occasion and while they could be mixed occasions, especially when a queen or princess was involved, such parties were dominated by women.

David Cressy notes that churching in the decades after the mid-sixteenth century Reformation was more about conformity to tradition than with any lingering notions of female pollution.[17] The ceremony by now belonged to a clear feminine tradition. Clerics agreed after the

Reformation on the month following childbirth, the grander month, as a period of physical recovery when the husband was excluded from the marital bed and lust was denied. During the sixteenth century a woman in childbed was considered green and therefore unready to return to the marital bed too soon. Prior to her churching she was expected to remain at home, refrain from sex and not participate in church rites. Many women were extremely relieved to forgo the marriage debt. Jane Seymour, sadly, did not live long enough to be churched and returned to the world.

Following the ritual of churching sexual relations between husband and wife could resume again as could normal domestic life.[18] According to Protestant Bishop Latimer, a woman before her purification 'is not meet to do such acts as other women, nor to have company with her husband ... To that end purification is kept and used, not to make superstition or holiness of it, as some do...women as I said afore, be as well in the favour of God before they be purified as after.'[19] In Protestant England the purification aspect of the event gave way to the recognition of a woman's need for rest and so a woman's much loved and needed tradition was preserved.

*   *   *

What if a woman or man wanted to avoid having children? Official medicine stayed away from this desire on the part of a couple. Folk medicine did not. For as long as people have had sex, despite serious Church objections, there have been methods of preventing pregnancy.

First up is the condom, or Venus glove as it was known at the time, which actually started as a form of venereal protection. Syphilis spread throughout Europe during the sixteenth century. It was a horrible disease and medical cures just as terrible. It was first recorded in Naples in 1495. *De Morbo Callus*, written in 1514, describes the progression of the disease: it caused skin lesions on its victim, lesions on bones and it attacked the brain in its later stages. An unpleasant secondary symptom is the loss of bodily hair. Mercury, which was used to deal with its symptoms, was ground, drunk, injected or applied to its sores and resulted in further hair loss, swollen gums and rotting teeth. Gabriele Falloppio (1623–1562) tried to fight the advance of the 'French disease' as it quickly became known (or 'English disease' in France) by advocating a fabric sheath fitted around the glands of the penis to prevent transmission. The sheath had to be soaked in a mix of wine, ashes, mercury, wood shavings and salt. The problem was that he instructed that the wrap be applied after sex rather than keeping it in place during sex. It would cleanse the penis of infection. Naturally, it was useless.[20]

Condoms came to be used as rudimentary methods of preventing pregnancy and were generally made of fish gut and were washed and reused. These would have been tied to the penis by a ribbon or fine string. There was a plethora of other rudimentary and bizarre methods of contraception. A lemon slice could be used as a cervical cap. Avicenna, the Arabic physician, as early as the eleventh century suggested the pulp of pomegranate mixed with alum made a useful pessary which could be inserted before coitus and a second pessary used afterwards. Alum was an efficient spermicide and also it made the mucus membrane of the vagina contract. Alum could even restore the vagina stretched by childbirth back to a normal size. Rock salt mixed with an oily material was yet another method believed to destroy male sperm.[21]

Other methods of contraception used at the time included a sponge inserted into the vagina or a plug of wool soaked with honey or wine to form a barrier. Drinking tincture of lead might introduce sterility but it could give rise to poisoning. Likewise, eating seeds of the castor oil plant was a dangerous, poisonous notion. Those desperate to prevent conception often used magical medicine. One recipe was marrow powdered and made into an infusion. Another was finely ground leaves of barren-wort taken in wine for five days after the menses to prevent conception. Its roots caused sterility. Pulverised berries of ivy drunk after purification could also bring about sterility. An infusion of marjoram taken during the menses could introduce sterility for a month as could the oil of pea taken regularly.[22]

The practice of *coitus interruptus* had long been a method of contraception but it was not condoned by the Church. In fact, wasting one's seed was considered almost as sinful as ending a life already in existence. Saint Thomas Aquinas was a Dominican Friar whose views were adopted by Catholic Church. These were set out in 1261 in *Summa Theologica* in three parts and reflect the Church's attitude towards birth control. Anything that hindered the generation of offspring was considered as taboo.[23] According to Genesis 9:7 the birth of children was essential and would remain central as humans were to 'increase and multiply.' One must remember that in this period the Church, ironically, considered female orgasm medically desirable and legitimate because if a woman had an orgasm she was, it believed, more likely to conceive a child.[24] There is no evidence that most women were supposed to be frigid in this period and there is none from medical literature or from sayings or proverbs either about the 'natural lustiness of women.'[25] It is easy to conclude that for many the Church view on this was often ignored.

Fear of unwanted pregnancy existed in all classes of people. Henry VIII's fifth wife, Katherine Howard, was famously reported to have said 'a woman might meddle with a man and yet conceive no child unless she would herself.'[26] A man was expected to have gained sexual experience before marriage. Fornication and adultery were exclusively male prerogatives even though women were considered by the Church as more lustful in attitude and also more fickle than men. The strictest standards of sexual behaviour were imposed on women and enforced by all the legal, moral and religious pressures society could impose. Women were the sexual property of men and a high value was attached to female chastity in the marriage market. After all, as mentioned above, there could be no doubts about the legitimacy of an heir.

In ancient Greek medicine the word 'hysteria', which described a feminine illness, came from the word uterus. It was attached to the notion of a 'wandering womb'. This was a valid medical state associated with childbirth, referring to a displaced womb. Practitioners needed to wrangle the womb back in place to its original position. It was not an unusual practice to drive the womb back down by waving the foul smells created by burning feathers, wool or linen over a woman. Equally, sweet-smelling spices and herbs were used to fumigate the vagina and tempt the womb down.[27]

Urine, as a diagnostic tool, was shaken and stirred. Another odd consultation chart carried by doctors was known as a 'penis tree'. It usually showed a wheel of fortune sprouting from a tree. Each branch of the tree showed a different broad diagnosis of illness. The outer layer offered colourful descriptions that could be matched to the urine's sample shade.[28]

The Tudor view of gender and sexuality possessed a degree of duality. On the one hand there was the elegance of courtly love, and on the other, to our twenty-first century minds, an eroticism as suggested by the doctor's urine chart depicting a penis tree. The significance of penis and womb was understandable because, of course, reproduction was the major purpose of sex. No wonder that Henry VIII, who was expert at the game of courtly love, was overjoyed to have produced a much longed for male heir with his third wife, Jane Seymour.

## A Summary of Tudor Childbirth Beliefs

During the medieval and Tudor eras pain relief in childbirth was illegal. One midwife was burned in 1591 for using opium for assisting labour. A woman had little choice but to trust in the midwife and in remedies handed down for centuries for help with childbirth.[1] Here are a few remedies used in the sixteenth century to ease childbirth anxiety and a number of rituals associated with pregnancy.

As her time approached the expectant mother might 'Rub the belly with powdered ants' eggs or/and try tying a piece of wild ox skin about the thigh of the mother about to give birth.' This might bring her good fortune during her labour. 'Sprinkle the bedsheets with holy water and close the door against daylight for some weeks as labour approaches' to keep devils from lurking about the birthing chamber.

A typical 'lying-in period' could last a month for a well-off lady, during which time she would not leave the chamber. She was veiled to be purified and perhaps she would undertake a pilgrimage to a Madonna's shrine to leave offerings of thanks for a safe birth. These offerings might be eggs, herbs, money and jewels. Peasant women, on the other hand, gave birth in barns, the cottage or in the fields and returned to work almost immediately.

Natural light was not permitted into her chamber for three days as birth was believed to strain the mother's eyesight. During seclusion one window in the birthing chamber was left uncovered; otherwise all windows were blacked out. This was designed to keep devils out as well as to keep the chamber secluded and warm. Cupboards were stocked with wine, food and spices to revive the labouring mother during her ordeal. Daily supplies and meals were deposited at the chamber door. This isolation was physical and symbolic.[2]

The Tudors believed in what the stars foretold. In 1490 Henry VII was presented with the translation of a work by the Italian astrologer, Guido Bonatti, outlining the influence of heavenly bodies at the exact time of a child's birth. Medical diagnosis was made in terms of the four humours. Female illnesses were treated by balancing or purging the body to remove bad influences that could weaken the child. The expectant mother could anticipate an enema or blood-letting.

When birth pains began the gossips – the name given to the female attendants –would follow folkloric rituals. Mothers would remove all fastenings, rings, buckles, bracelets and laces that might imitate a state of strangulation on her body lest this might be transferred to the child.

No one present in the birthing chamber could cross legs, arms, or fingers during birthing. Brandy distilled and mixed with marjoram and saffron might help contractions if rubbed on the labouring woman's stomach.

The pregnant mother might tie a magic girdle with pieces of paper inscribed with charms for protection about her belly. Cowrie shells, which are shaped like the vulva, might be tied there instead or as well as to bring her good luck. An eagle stone containing a smaller stone to create a rattling sound when shaken was believed to alleviate pain and prevent miscarriage and was often worn during late pregnancy. Wax discs stamped with an image of the lamb and flag, blessed by the Pope, were believed to offer protection from sudden death or demons' malevolence during birthing.

Herbs and flowers were used in various ways to help lessen the pains of contractions. Oil of lilies, wild thyme and musk may have helped ease pains. Powdered eel liver, virgin's hair, ale and red cow's milk might be on offer. Enemas were given to aid dilation and occasionally sub fumigation might channel herbal vapours into the womb. Special powders could induce sneezing as this was believed to help expel the child.

Reading the gospels during delivery was a well-used method to ensure all went smoothly. A reliquary placed in the birthing chamber would display a range of holy items such as holy bones, phials of a saint's blood, tears of milk and shards of the true cross. Pre-Reformation mothers believed in the comforting presence of saints and the power of prayer during labour.

In 1425 a prayer book containing an English rubric and Latin prayer written apparently by St Peter for labouring women was used by attendants and midwives, assuming they learned the prayer or could read.[2] The benefit of charm and prayer being in repetition which can help to concentrate the mind. The word 'abracadabra' was, in fact, a popular chant. A tenth-century charm in Occitan was often recited by midwives to create a rhythm in sympathy with a woman's contractions and establish regular breathing.[3]

A 'groaning chair' allowed the midwife to help with the delivery while another attendant helped the pregnant mother brace against pain by pressing down on the top of the womb. Rope tourniquets were sometimes used to aid expulsion. There were no forceps in the early Tudor era; these were an Elizabethan invention and not widely used for another century.

The newborn's umbilical cord was cut and anointed, possibly with frankincense if it could be afforded, or with powdered aloe. This occurred before the child was washed with a mixture of herbs, wine, milk and rubbed with butter, oil of almonds, roses or nuts to close their pores to prevent harm from air.

The baby would be tightly swaddled and given a spoonful of wine with sugar. The placenta was delivered through a mini labour during which the mother's womb was again massaged until the afterbirth was delivered. Once it had been, the midwives would check that no remaining fragments were left to cause fatal haemorrhaging later. At last the mother was washed down with a clean sponge and permitted rest but not sleep for a few hours.

\* \* \*

Superstition, custom and religious practice permeated medieval and early Tudor consciousness. However, by 1540 many of the old customs were outlawed as the Reformation took hold. Midwives would now have to rethink the methods previously used.

The Cult of the Virgin Mary, popular with pregnant mothers, was particularly attacked because it represented idolatry's excesses and the suspicion of Catholic guarantees of salvation. The specific misogyny directed at these shrines was savage and sexually orientated. At Walsingham, a major pilgrimage site where pilgrims prayed for the safe delivery of children and gave thanks following a birth, the statue of the Virgin was removed and burned. It became known as 'Falsingham' and a new series of pilgrim badges was issued depicting saints and pilgrims in lewd poses to illustrate supposed sexual immorality of pilgrims. Our Lady of Woolpit, which had a healing spring, was nicknamed 'Lady of the

Foulpit', and Our Lady of Willesden was labelled 'a common paramour of baudy'. Mary herself was attacked by Bishop Latimer as possessing pride, arrogance and was bad-mannered because she reprimanded Jesus. Edward VI's tutor described the Church of Rome as 'An arrogant whore, a fornicator and an idolatress'.[4]

Women had taken comfort in the possession of images or icons of their favourite saints in the birthing chamber. After a 1535 proclamation was issued that all false images were to 'be utterly abolished, eradicated and erased out,' and there was to be no memory of idolatry in walls, glass windows or elsewhere. Thomas Cromwell ordered a systematic destruction referred to at the time as 'the long summer of iconoclasm'. Any girdles used for pregnant mothers and combs dedicated to St Mary Magdalen, St Dorothy and St Margaret were taken and destroyed. St Mary's red silk girdle was taken from Bruton in Somerset. The girdle at Westminster (said to have touched the original 'Girdle of Thomas' which was supposedly made and worn by the Madonna) long used by pregnant royalty, including Catherine of Aragon, Elizabeth of York and Margaret Tudor, was removed and destroyed. Injunctions of 1547 banned the use of rosaries, undertaking pilgrimages and prayers for particular saints associated with personal prayer and pregnant women.[5]

A birthing mother could not recite the rosary, have holy water cast upon her bed, allow the ringing of holy bells, or have candles blessed. Charms, witchcraft, sorcery, enchantments, invocations and soothsaying were decreed inventions of the devil, especially during labour. Old chants were replaced by new chants substituting female saints with male saints. Here is an example of a typical chant that came down through centuries.

> There are four corners to her bed
> Four angels at her head
> Matthew, Mark, Luke and John
> God bless the bed she lies upon
> New moon, new moon, God bless me
> God bless this house and family.

An embargo was imposed on growing or using herbs and flowers from monastic infirmary gardens, which were destroyed, leaving a significant gap in medical learning. Fake relics that existed and body parts collected as relics of saints may seem nonsensical now but they provided reassurance to prospective parents. It is true that many of these practices were corrupt, yet cultural changes took away comforts women had traditionally enjoyed during childbirth, comforts that provided them with a sense of control over a dangerous area of their lives. But these centuries-old traditions did not suddenly change women and for many, the outlawed practices simply went underground.[6]

# Chapter 4

# Attracting the Opposite Sex

It may surprise you that the Tudors cared about cleanliness despite the fact many did not bathe regularly. Henry VIII frequently took baths and had a new bathhouse constructed at Hampton Court for his personal use as well as a steam bath at Richmond palace. This new bath was made of wood but lined with a linen sheet to protect his posterior from catching splinters.[2] It was a marvellous feat of Tudor engineering and allowed water to flow into it from a tap fed by a lead pipe bringing water from a spring which was over three miles distant from the palace. Tudor engineers were clever enough to pass the pipe underneath the Thames river bed using gravity to create water pressure strong enough to spurt up two floors into the royal bathroom.

It was important to most Tudors not to stink, and particularly important not to smell unpleasant when contemplating relations with a lover.[3] Smelling like a beast was totally unacceptable to a Tudor because, ideally, humans should smell sweet. Of course, the Tudor world was less sanitised than our own world. Even so, people were not unaware of bad smells around them and they actually feared nasty pongs. Medicine taught that disease spread through miasma or foul smelling airs. Tudors also believed that sweet smells could be a key indicator of a person's moral state, never mind that smelling sweet could help when attracting a lover.

Bathing for most Tudors meant a dip in the river. For those dwelling in towns, bathing facilities such as bathhouses existed during the first few decades of the era. Crusaders had brought the habit of bathing back from the East, thereby making the idea of bathhouses popular.

Hygiene meant both cleaning oneself and one's clothes regularly. Just as the Church clamped down on sexual freedoms, it had opinions on bathing: heat could inflame the senses; and washing nude was a sign of vanity, even sexual corruption, so they often wore shirts while bathing.[4] *The Book of Nature* by John Russells advises scenting a bath with flowers and sweet green herbs to help cure ailments, attaching a medicinal element to the practice.⁵ Exotic perfumes such as civet and musk were used in soaps, as well as rose water, violet, lavender and camphor. For those who could afford scented soaps they were available.

Where public bathhouses went sex soon followed so it is no wonder the ever-critical Church complained. Tudor brothels were called 'stews' and 'to lather up' was an early sixteenth-century slang phrase for ejaculation which came from the notion that one could stew in hot water and steam within a bathhouse. It was as recently as the previous century that the City of London officially recognised the borough of Southwark as having the highest concentration of bathhouses in London. Ironically, this was an area owned by the Bishop of Winchester and since many bathhouses were also brothels their sex workers acquired the alternative name of Winchester Geese.

As the sixteenth century continued bathing fell into decline as new medical advice suggested it weakened the body. Cleaning the skin left it open to infection. This was considered an outside agency that drifted in the air like spores and which rose from places of putrefaction. The pores of the skin was one body area through which these nasty spores could enter and so medical advice determined that the skin needed to be preserved as a barrier. Pores were a secondary route into the body and the filth produced by the body must be removed completely and quickly to avoid reabsorption. It became important to wash your shirt and change it frequently to keep clean.

Linen shirts, smocks, under-breeches, hose, collars, coifs and skull caps all allowed the body total coverage. As a fabric, linen was very absorbent. It drew sweat and grease from the skin into the weave of the cloth. Since linen acted like a sponge, the Tudors thought it would draw out waste products from the body as well as improve the body's circulation, strengthen the constitution and even restore the balance of the humours.

Laundresses were popular during Tudor times, not just to keep linen washed but because the washerwomen were easily connected with sex.⁶ They were badly paid so in many cases sex work was a way to subsidise their income. The word lavender comes from the Latin *lavare* to wash and the word to launder derives from these sweet smelling flowers. Lavender grows all over Europe and as it was cheap and readily available it was used widely when washing clothing. Washerwomen sometimes became known as 'lavenders'. The sixteenth century poem *Ship of Fools* contains the following lines:

> Thou shalt be my lavender Laundress
> To Wash and keep all my gear
> Our two beds together shall be set
> Without any let.[7]

People used linen to scrub the body. The Tudor Gentleman, Sir Thomas Elyot, wrote a book in 1534 called *The Castel of Health*. He suggests an early morning hygiene regime to 'rubbe the body with a course lynnen clothe, first softly and easilye, and after that increase more and more, to a hard and swift rubbynge, untyll the flesh do swelle and to be somewhat ruddy and that not only down ryghte, but also overthrart and round.' Rubbing vigorously after exercise could draw the body's toxins out through open pores and the rough linen cloth would carry them away.[8] According to Ruth Goodman writing in *How to be a Tudor*, most people only owned two or three sets of underwear. They occasionally turned up in Tudor inventories and linens would often be recorded in wills as bequeathed to others.

Goodman tells us how she followed a Tudor body cleansing regime for a period of three months while living in modern society. No one complained or even noticed a sweaty smell. She wore natural fibre on top of the linen underwear but took neither a shower nor a bath for the whole period. When she recorded *The Monastery Farm* for television, she only changed her linen smock once weekly and her hose three times over six months and she still did not pong.[9] Tudor England was not a place where everyone smelled as sweetly as most people who shower daily today but its people generally managed not to stink. Of course, the past did smell differently but being clean and sweet smelling certainly did matter to many Tudors.

In 1485 only a few hundred people in England could afford essential oils which arrived during the Crusades. Perfume for most people originated from natural sources such as posies of violets, lavender bags and smoke from herbs burning over a fire. Sir Thomas More is known to have had a rosemary bush planted beneath his study window so its pleasant scent wafted up towards him as he worked. Lavender was often placed in bedrooms, tucked into the straw of a bolster or hung in bunches

on bed posts so that its calming nature might induce relaxation. Rue and
Tansey were known as insecticides and were strewn on floors and mixed
into bedstraw. Marjoram was stowed amongst daytime clothing to induce
a merry state of mind. Bags of rose petals mixed with dried Orris root
might also influence one's mood positively, and rose oil on the skin was
also considered to act as an aphrodisiac.[10]

The smell from an essential oil, especially rose oil or musk, could create
a sensual feeling, but, as we have seen, these were only affordable for
the very wealthiest in society. On the positive side for those liking to
smell sweet, a better knowledge of distillation spread among apothecaries
and the educated elite and so a price drop gradually followed as home
production of perfumes increased. Apothecaries would cleverly produce
distilled waters which were much cheaper than oils. These distilled
waters were consequently used in foods and medicines, as scented hand
washes, and the delightful new scents were widely sprinkled on linens.[11]

As well as owning an aphrodisiac quality, roses were thought to have
a warming, strengthening nature and therefore could quicken the blood.
Even their smell was considered arousing. Rose oil made by distillation
became popular at King Henry's court, not just to arouse the senses or
because the smell was pleasant, but because the rose was a symbol of
the Tudor dynasty. Henry VIII purchased huge quantities of rose waters
and perfumes for his personal use and to sprinkle around his hall during
festive occasions. Beautiful casting bottles filled with oil of roses made
a much appreciated sexy gift at the Tudor court. A casting bottle would
use oil of thyme, lemons, cloves and a grain of civet worked together with
distilled rose water.

Rose oil eventually lost popularity by Elizabeth I's reign when musk,
civet and ambergris competed with rose as the perfume most valued at
court. Could this be because once rose oil became so readily available it
lost its exclusivity value?

Another way for a Tudor to smell sweet was to have herbs and spices
worked into a ball of wax or lump of resin to make a pomander. The
pomander was placed in a perforated box, suspended by a cord and worn
over clothing. If a woman wore her pomander on a long cord suspended
from her girdle it would knock against her skirt as she moved, creating a
pleasant wafting scent about her person.

Von der Ehe. LXXXIII

God Joining Man and Woman in Marriage by Heinrich Stayner of Augsburg (*Public Domain*)

Adam and Eve by Albrecht Dürer (*Rijksmuseum*)

The Wedding of Prince Arthur and Catherine of Aragon from a Flemish Tapestry. (*Courtesy of Wiki Commons*)

Courtship Gift Gloves. (*Author's own photo taken at Shakespeare's House, Stratford on Avon*)

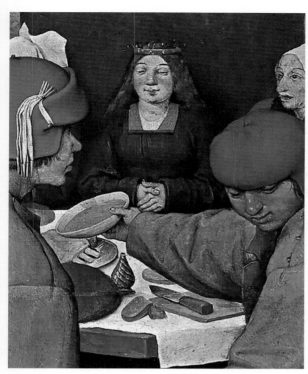

Peasant Wedding, section of painting by Pieter Brughel, elder, 1567. (*Elizabeth Chadwick, courtesy of Wiki Commons, original Kunsthistoriches Museum, Wein*)

Tudor Bed replica. (*Author's own photo taken at Shakespeare's House, Stratford on Avon*)

Wolf Hall. (*Courtesy of The Friends of Wolf Hall*)

Jane Seymour. (*Author's own picture, The Mauritshus Collection, The Hague*)

St Katherine, Bernardini Luini 1482–1532, National Museum of Azerbaijan. (*Courtesy of Wiki Commons*)

A visit to a Brothel, The Brunswick Monogamist, Brothel, Stadel Museum. (*Courtesy of Wiki Commons*)

Communal Bathing in a Bath House. (*Wiki Commons*)

Idealised portrait of a Courtesan, An unknown lady in the guise of Flora, Bartolomeo Veneto, 1520, Stadelsches Gallery, Frankfurt. (*Courtesy of Wiki Commons*)

Birth of Venus by Sandro Botticelli. (*Courtesy of B.L on Flickr*)

Lady with an Ermine by
Leonardo da Vinci. (*National
Museum, Krakow, Flickr/ Wiki
Commons*)

Dynastic Portrait of Henry VIII and his Family by Holbein, Hampton Court Palace. The king is seated centre beneath a canopy of state flanked by Jane Seymour and Prince Edward. (*Courtesy of Flickr*)

Portrait of a Gentleman in his Study by Lotto, Academia Venice. (*Courtesy of Wiki Commons*)

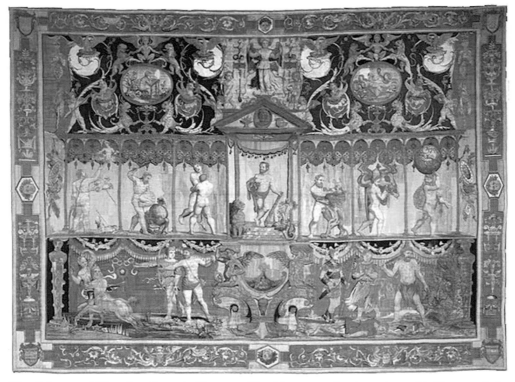

The Labours of Hercules, Brussels Tapestry. The labours are in three tiers with Fame and the Grotesques above. It was recorded in the Westminster Palace Inventory of the 1540s.

Medallion showing Catherine of Aragon on Henry VIII's writing desk, close up, V&A collection, 1525. (*Courtesy of Wiki Commons*)

Henry VIII's writing desk, V&A collection, 1525. (*Courtesy of Wiki Commons*)

Considering that Tudors used all sorts of convenient places to urinate, the pomander was considered a necessary accessary at court. Rather than walking to a 'House of Easement', courtiers had a habit of relieving themselves in fireplaces and even in passages. Servants were even guiltier of this unpleasant habit. Gentlemen and gentlewomen kept chamber pots within their personal apartments at court. An excavated Tudor piss pot on display at Hampton Court still contains traces of genuine Tudor urine.

The nobility were more fortunate and owned garberobes attached to their rooms. These garderobes, or stool rooms, were occasionally places for illicit Tudor trysts. Particularly noteworthy was a tryst between Katheryn Howard and Thomas Culpepper, her alleged lover, during the Northern Progress, which heralded her undoing. They were known to have concealed themselves in her garderobe.[12]

*    *    *

Tudors washed and used scent, but what about hair, especially pubic hair? They were very interested in hair and not just that on the head. By the sixteenth century, texts with beauty advice became popular. In 1532 one famous Venetian beauty manual had a recipe for a homemade depilatory cream: 'Boil together a solution of one pint of arsenic and eighth of a pint of quicklime. Go to the baths or a hot room and smear medicine over the area to be depilated. When the skin feels hot, wash quickly with hot water so the flesh doesn't come off.'[13]

In 1528 Francisco Delicado's *La Lozana Andaluza*, a publication about a Roman sex worker, describes whores who pluck their eyebrows and others who shave their pubic parts. One wonders if in Southwark bathhouses, a Londoner might be offered similar treatment. The same writer speaks of accidentally burning off all the hair from the privates of a lady from Bologna and healing the burn with butter.

Shaving the pubes has happened throughout history, and the Tudors were just as involved in such beauty activity as their predecessors. A practical reason for removing pubic hair was, of course, the occurrence of pubic lice. This could only be got rid of by shaving. Then there was syphilis, first recorded in Naples in 1495. An unpleasant symptom of secondary-stage syphilis is entire hair loss and patchy pubes were a sign of this disease.[14]

Pubic hair, on the other hand, was much admired during the Renaissance and among some, if not all Tudors. The slang words for pubic hair during the era included 'feathers', 'fleece', 'flush', 'moss', 'plush', 'plume', and, interestingly, 'the admired abode'.[15] The plural *malkin* or *merkin* appeared during the mid-fifteenth century. Malkin was a word for a mop but merkin, a derivative, was also a term for a pubic hair wig which might be used to conceal hair loss due to syphilis.[16]

This brings us to Tudor grooming. Combs, made out of box wood or cow horn, bone and ivory, were double-sided, possessing fine teeth on one side especially to remove fleas and lice. Tudors combed their hair at least once daily. Since they desired to be free of lice and fleas, the amorous would have used a fine comb as an effective method of removing head lice and preventing nits. Washing the hair was not usual except in summer or in warmer climes. Hot water could open up facial pores and for this reason scalp hair was generally rinsed in cold, herb-scented water. Nostradamus, who was a French court physician at one point in his life, published a book of recipes in 1552. He claimed that the very fashionable golden colour was possible, as was dyeing hair black. Since both his recipes meant washing the hair with lyre to dissolve grease, hair treated in this way could become brittle and the scalp could be harmed by this harsh soap.[17] The treatment was dangerous for the skin but a sensible warning would go unheeded by any vain lady wanting to be a popular blond or by an aging courtier desiring black hair.

What about personal hygiene? Douching can be traced back to the ancient world. However, the practice was not used during the early modern period and did not return in popularity until the nineteenth century. The vulva and vagina has its individual signature scent unique to its owner, a scent that can spike the male's testosterone level, playing its part in sexual arousal. In a subliminal way the Tudors knew instinctively that douching or washing out the vagina was unnecessary. It was sexier to smell whiffy in that area or perhaps they picked up on the fact the vagina is self-cleaning. In *The Tortula*, still popular during this period and written during the twelfth century in Salerno, it is mentioned that a severe odour often found in the vagina was unpleasant for sexual intercourse and might create a distaste to male sexual partners who would likely leave the coupling unfinished. A prescription used by Muslim women suggests a redolent water mixture that constricts the vagina and represses the odour. These instructions include detailed instructions on how to apply the concoction before intercourse using a powder that the lady is to rub on her chest, breasts and genitalia. She is to wash her partner's privates using a cloth sprinkled with the same sweet-smelling powder. An example suggests taking powder of blackberry and placing it inside to constrict the vagina.[18]

Sweet-smelling breath was valued by Tudors. No one really wanted their lover to experience stinking breath while kissing. A Tudor morning hygiene regime included rinsing one's mouth out with clean water and they frequently washed their hands and faces before dining. After eating, many fastidious Tudors used tooth picks to remove fragments of food. Disposable toothpicks were available and purchased by the wealthy as Tudor accounts prove. Powders for cleaning the teeth combined breath sweetening with tooth whitening.

The Tudors collected soot from a wax candle by holding the candle against a pane of glass or the polished surface of an earthenware pot. The soot could be rubbed directly onto the teeth, acting as a tooth cleaner. Equally, chalk and salt, or ashes from rosemary wood gathered into a small pouch might be rubbed all around the mouth. Tooth cloths were used to wipe the gums, teeth and tongue before the mouth was rinsed out. Barber surgeons offered a tooth-scraping service, and, would you believe, tooth bleaching with 'aqua fortis'. This whitener was created from a distillation of an alkali or acid. On the downside, aqua fortis could destroy gums and strip the tooth enamel.[19] If not too worried about the future the young in love could kiss with the knowledge they were kissing a pleasantly clean mouth and the Tudor gentleman could flash white teeth at his mistress when smiling.

*   *   *

The king may have possessed his own bathhouse but most city subjects visited public bathhouses that were sometimes used by men and women together. The bathhouses were a social experience and by the fifteenth century bath feasting in town bathhouses became 'as common as going out to a restaurant four centuries later.'[20] Tudors enjoyed medieval stories and legends. In *The Arthurian Legends*, beloved by the Henrician court, taking a bath was written as an erotic experience. *The Romance of the Rose*, a famous medieval poem, includes a bathtub in which Venus steamed the ladies and the writer remarks, 'the young man who has no one to teach him, takes a perilous bath.'

Boraccio's *Decameron* contains satires of lecherous monks and nuns in erotic situations involving the bathtub.[21] Nuns famously left convents to go on pilgrimage to spas in fifteenth-century Germany, which were also sites and springs dedicated to saints. Clerics are recorded as having cavorted at Baden. Late medieval literature and art often suggests baths as part of amorous foreplay and ecclesiastical writers recognised the popularity of bathing while using spiritual analogies in their writings. *The Life of Saint Katherine of Alexandria*, scribed by John Capgrave during the fifteenth century, tells us that Jesus ordered Saint Katherine to be washed clean before her mystical wedding.

Ritual washing was also about purity and beauty within the secular world. Images represent a kind of baptism and marriage ritual present or imagined in the life of a saint. Capgrave writes:

> It is a goodly usage, sothely to seye
> Who shall be wedded to a duke or king
> Before her wedding to have a bathing
> For to make her sweet, for to make her clean
> Else might she rein in full great offence.[22]

A Luttrell Psalter held in The British Library shows an image of a haloed woman bathing another haloed woman in a tub. This could be the Virgin being washed by Saint Anne. The Wenceslas Bible contains images where the king appears, sometimes naked, in a tub being washed by female bathing attendants wearing see-through white shifts. The images on this occasion could concern childlessness; the maidens' presence representative of virtue and fertility. The Czech king's two marriages were childless so he may have been trying for increased virility.[23]

Artistic images from the period suggest baths were draped with sheets raised to form a tent like a steam bath. An attendant, female, would rub herbs into the body or, alternatively, the bather might soak in herbs. All seems delightful. However, there was also an association with prostitution hanging around the Southwark bathhouses. A shock for bathhouse proprietors descended upon them during 1546. In this year, the bathhouses of London were closed down to the sound of proclamations and trumpets. Reasons for the closure went further than the belief that germs might enter the skin's pores, or even that communal bathing was immoral. The real reason was because syphilis was running through the city stews like wildfire. People were worried that the disease could pollute bathwater, get into the bather's pores and infect them. At this time, holy wells and spas were also closed down. As the Reformation swept across England, they were considered idolatrous and dedicated to saints. There was no place for such spas within the context of Church reform.

Baths were, from the 1540s, to become medicinal rather than for cleansing. People still washed their hands, faces and feet regularly and most likely their more private parts. Being clean and smelling sweet still mattered. In 1540 Henry VIII claimed he could not consummate his marriage with Anne of Cleves because of the evil smells and unpleasant airs about her person. Clearly, she was not too keen on bathing, or perhaps she simply possessed a strong unpleasant body odour.

# Chapter 5

# Dress to Impress

Attracting the opposite sex was not just about smelling pleasant and clean. During the sixteenth century a rich flowering in fashion, literature and painting evolved at the Tudor court and also amongst the wealthy minor nobility, as well as rising middle and merchant classes. Renaissance thought led to a new self-consciousness and sense of personal individuality. During this century, self-fashioning, the notion of creating oneself as well-read and noticeable, was embodied by the dress worn by Henry VIII and in the personality and dress of Henry Howard, Earl of Surrey. Both men were extremely vain and both dressed to impress in a contrasting manner. Henry VIII was a colourful peacock, whilst Surrey was a poet, darkly intense and brooding, as reflected in his dress sense.[1]

It is a well-known fact that King Henry VIII liked to dress fashionably and loved disguise. Henry resembled his grandfather, Edward IV, in looks. He was handsome. The poet John Skelton (1460–1529) called him a 'fresh Adonis'. Just after the seventeen-year-old prince inherited the throne in 1509, Lord Mountjoy, writing to Desiderius Erasmus before the young king's coronation, said Henry VIII was a 'new auspicious star,' who had 'already something of royalty in his demeanour.' The new King was highly intelligent, artistic, well-read, athletic and handsome, beautifully and expensively dressed. In 1504 the Spanish ambassador wrote that Henry was a child who 'deserves all love'.[2] All was optimistic in 1509 when the young King and his beautiful bride, Catherine of Aragon, were crowned.

In appearance Henry was clean-shaven, fair-haired, tall and athletic, 'the handsomest potentate I ever set eyes on,' according to another contemporary. The new King was above average height with straight, short, auburn hair, a round, pretty face and rosebud mouth. Henry dressed extravagantly, making the most of his position of kingship and his good looks. When his looks faded as he grew older, the portrait painter Hans

Holbein ensured he still looked his best while preserving a true likeness. There were no large glass mirrors during the early 1500s, but there were many polished metal mirrors available which added a deceptive glow and gentleness to the image. Henry owned a number of these and it is probable the likeness he observed in them as he aged looked softer than his looks were in reality.[3]

Henry adored silks, velvets and other beautiful but expensive fabrics such as sarsinet and damask. In 1509 he appeared to be a perfect Renaissance prince. During this era the male calf is noted as an important aspect of beauty and so the competitive, vain Henry enjoyed displaying his thighs and his calves. In his youth, he possessed a shapely calf which was enhanced by the clothing he liked to wear, in particular coats that could be swept aside to allow a glimpse of his thigh.

Portraits of Henry show him standing six feet tall, square, staring out from the canvass wearing doublet, hose, coat and gown. As well as showing off a well-formed thigh, Henry's gown revealed sumptuous layers of fabric beneath his coat, particularly when it was worn hanging open. Extravagant courtly dressing was about power during the Tudor era and power exuded sex. Suggestive costuming such as showing off the neat thigh also was about virility and this was very important to Henry VIII personally, since he desired an heir and a spare.

Where royalty led, others followed. Doublets and sexy hose soon attracted attention across the social strata. The man's hose, worn beneath the gown, was suggestive as it followed the contours of the body, permitting the wearer a slim appearance. The doublet provided body warmth, but it also held up the hose. The coat became the alternative to the loose gown that had been popular during Henry VII's era. A coat was worn for more formal occasions such as attending church, court appearances, weddings, guild events and for extra warmth when outside in cooler weather.

The hose stretched from waist to toe. A tailor would punch a row of paired holes around the doublet inside waistline so hose could be tied to the doublet either tightly or loosely. If hose was joined too loosely, disaster could follow as there would be bagging or exposure. Back ties might be left undone for comfort but the front points would always be tightened. If the wearer bent over too far and the back ties worked too loose the effect could resemble that of builder's bum. Hose were two separate stockings.[4]

They needed to show the limb off perfectly and never show any wrinkles, a major Tudor fashion faux pas.

The young men at Henry's court usually wore tight-fitting hose to enhance their male physical beauty, but fashion came at a cost. Hose could prove uncomfortable. With the recently fashionable footed hose there could be pressure on the knees if all was too tight. Fitted hose could permit a little bagginess at the knees to accommodate movement and if a garter was tied just below the knees confining bagginess to the knee area leg-wear could appear slim and snug against the young man's lower leg. He would look fashionably and attractively clad. In this way Henry could flash his perfect calves.

In paintings and manuscript work young Renaissance men appear utterly gorgeous, jewelled and colourful. The images aim to show beauty as a signifier of inward purity and Godliness, and therefore nothing to do with sex. But they *are* sexy, and doubtless they appeared so during the sixteenth century, depending on who was looking. Hose colours were significant: green hose suggested youthful vigour while red suggested passion. Fashions shown on illustrations are often outrageous, suggestive of the exotic, foreign and mythical.

As Henry's reign progressed, and shorter coats became fashionable, the protective codpiece men wore became even more noticeable than ever. The codpiece was originally related to the Highlander's sporran and is related to the sportsman's jockstrap of later times, but it undoubtedly possessed a flamboyance all of its own. The codpiece created a sense of manly display, even from under a full suit of armour.[5]

The codpiece began in the Middle Ages as a mere limp triangular flap to deal with the embarrassing absence of a covering, intended to cover that revealing gap between the two separate pieces of men's stockings. It was also protective if created from metal and worn with armour for battle. By the sixteenth century the codpiece had developed into a statement of high fashion, therefore Tudor codpieces were individualised and accessorised and often made of luxurious decorated materials complete with ribbons and bobbles.[6] Tudor men could mix and match their codpieces. A manly man could also strut around court in a garment that mimicked male genitals, drawing attention to them and exaggerating them to an absurd degree. His codpiece might be stuffed with straw to make it shapelier. Its hollow chamber had another use since it could also protect the lovely outer surface of stockings from the nasty sullying mercury-based ointment used to treat syphilis. It was also useful as a pocket. Money might be deposited within it because the wearer might need to pay an admirer. A kerchief could be tucked in the codpiece to facilitate some hasty mopping up operation. Amusingly, the codpiece sometimes served as a pincushion: men's attire in the sixteenth century was so complicated, with many folds and wrappings around, sweepings over, tuckings, and overlappings, that pins might come in handy.[7] The codpiece was daring, solid and padded. The larger the codpiece the more status was implied by its wearer.

Cod was slang for scrotum. We also have the expression 'a man's crown or family jewels', referring to the pocket where coins or jewels could be stored. Just imagine reaching into the codpiece pocket for a jewel to give to a lover or mistress or even to pay a prostitute. Henry's enormous codpiece emphasised his desired virility and capacity for providing England with heirs so he was never shy of strutting it about. It forms the centre-piece of Holbein's drawing, *The Whitehall Cartoon*, which gives us Henry's definitive image. A suit of armour belonging to Henry displayed in the Tower of London has an enormous metal codpiece. During past eras, female visitors to the Tower would stick pins in its lining hoping it would increase their own virility.[8]

Holbein was extremely clever at capturing true likenesses as well as evoking richness and majesty. He flattered Henry, showing him in huge magnificence decked out in jewels, from rubies set in his collar to gems on his cap and worked into his doublet. This richness had to be displayed in portraiture because it was Henry's identity. The Henrician court was one of the wealthiest in Europe and Henry himself was a patron of the arts. His aggressive stance in portraiture portrayed his majestic presence, legs apart, directly facing the viewer. Yet again, this was another strategy aimed to reinforce the strength of the Tudor dynasty. Layers of material broadened King Henry's shoulders. His clothing showed a square silhouette tapering down to slimmer legs, leading the eye to the central royal importance of the procreative area, and, importantly, to Henry's codpiece that held the potential for England's future ruler.[9] Henry's opulence and rich surroundings, particularly when depicted as a still-young, handsome man in his forties, confirmed his wealth, power and virility. It is interesting that Henry's armour in the Tower of London shows a man with shorter legs than in the portraits, perhaps more true to reality. Holbein's genius knew how to please.

Henry was always first to view luxury silks and velvets introduced into England. He imported materials from around the world and never wore the same ensemble twice when on show at a special occasion. Statutes of apparel during his reign forbad colours such as purple, gold, silver and crimson to be worn by the lower classes. Even so, the introduction of new textiles and exciting new fabric mixes brought greater textile varieties and new fashions into England that appealed to the merchant classes as well as court. At this time new fashions originated in Germany, Italy and Spain. They included velvet hats as well as velvet mantles trimmed with fur, and doublets of silk mixes with a deal of puffing and slashing cut into the fabric. The *simar* became a must have. It was a robe, a little like an ecclesiastical coat, embroidered and extravagant. Henry wears a *simar* in his later portraits.

Holbein liked to use plain, darker backgrounds for his paintings which highlighted jewellery detail. Jewellery was significant at the Tudor court and very desirable as gifts. Gems represented portable wealth and therefore power that could travel about with the wearer. Flash them as much as possible on fingers, around necks, or as brooches on hats, displaying power and sex appeal. Mirrors, as mentioned above, were in vogue. Both Francis I and Henry VIII were avid mirror collectors and vain monarchs, and always competitive. During their meeting on the Cloth of Gold in 1521 a parade of wealth was displayed to ensure an alliance between France and England (and England's safety). A later painting of this majestic occasion shows the two kings holding gloves, wearing flat caps decorated with feathers, badges and buttons, with parures – jewellery that matched their clothing. Henry's codpiece is outlined by the rings on his index finger pointing towards it.

Portraits could not hide Henry's later deterioration, but nonetheless he maintained high standards of dress, allowing his powerful status and reflecting his virile image to dominate the canvas, just as it did in younger images of the King.

Henry VIII loved dressing up in exotic clothing. As well as Eastern fabrics his wardrobe contained French, Italian, Spanish and Turkish styles. He adored slippers, shoes and a variety of fancy costumes. He kept all his own costumes from masques he starred in and owned Turkish coats of blue satin. A charge made against Anne Boleyn at her trial in 1536 was that she laughed at Henry's attire.[10]

Women wore simpler clothing than men during the early Tudor period. The smock was the garment women wore nearest the skin and it suggested modesty and comfort. Its linen absorbed sweat. Importantly, it was regularly changed. The smock was sewn from rectangles with triangular pieces (gores) at the side allowing fullness at the hips. A lady wore no knickers, though Italian women wore under-drawers by the Renaissance era, a fashion that was mostly associated with courtesan dress and at the time very sexy. Just think of the titillation they provided, especially if pretty under-drawers crept into the brothels of Southwark. There is a hint of cross dressing if women wore them, as referred to in another chapter.[11]

Women's hose followed. Unlike men's hose, it was never temptingly on show and was shorter, more like knee socks. Hose was also made of linen. Only wealthy ladies could afford sexy silk knitted hose. Woollen hose, a winter alternative, had an advantage because wool resisted feet bacteria and could be worn for longer before laundering. Both linen and wool allow sweat to evaporate quickly. It was appealing for a woman to have a clean smock, clean hands and clean feet and to smell clean. Smock and hose together provided a barrier between the skin and the outer world of dirt and disease.

The hose was held up by garters tied above the knee. Garters traditionally were stolen from a bride after the wedding feast and tossed to the groomsmen, a little like tossing a bridal bouquet today. The lucky recipient might hope to be the next to marry.

A kirtle covered the smock. It was a full-length dress, sleeved and laced together, fitted above the waist and it then flared out. In Tudor times a woman's dress consisted of two parts. A gown, the outer layer, was made of better cloth than the under kirtle. A kirtle is an undergown. Gowns also had lower collars than kirtles so the upper part of the kirtle bodice would show. The gown had shorter sleeves. In this way the undergarment, the kirtle, could fetchingly be shown off. Extravagant gowns of rich fabrics were always worn at court, to functions and on formal occasions. Kirtles could be really tricky to remove. Back-lacing kirtles usually required maids to remove them, tempting and teasing for the lover's fingers. A kirtle could be side-laced or front-laced. The kirtle was a useful working garment. It was warm and close-fitting, and could shield the wearer from heat and sparks from the fireplace.

Tudor women wore their linen shift in bed and changed it to a clean one in the morning. Men wore an undershirt to bed or slept nude. As well as to provide warmth in bed, everyone wore a form of nightcap to keep devils out of their ears while they slept. Henry VIII provided Anne Boleyn with nightdresses. One was of black satin bound with black taffeta and edged with black velvet. It was possibly a comfortable, loose, hooded garment, more like a dressing gown, which she wore about her chamber over clothing rather than actually in bed.[12]

Women' hair was combed out and worn loose on their wedding day to show off their maidenly innocence. A head of luxuriant locks was considered sexual, so after marriage the married woman's hair was controlled using tapes and laces, reflecting societal rules towards wives and sex. Married sex was, one must repeat, about begetting children and being an obedient wife. However, vanity slipped through the barriers, as ever it does. Tudor ladies used jewelled pins to secure the braids and pairs of gorgeous, and valuable, silver pins are recorded in bequests associated with wills.

Vanity dictated a more rigid fashion than simply twisting hair up into a bun. Plaiting two bunches of hair with braids crossed at the neck, brought up and crossed at the top and then taken back round again with laces tied together resulted in a fashion which, if not sexy, could be adapted and teasingly glimpsed below the final headdress. Since a woman's hair was her crowning glory, padding was often used when a long, bound braid was drawn up and coiled on the top of the head and the cap placed on top. This provided an illusion of sensual volume, provocative beneath the headdress.

Headgear became interesting during the Tudor period. A pointed gabled look was the fashion for the headdress during the early decades of the sixteenth century and remained so until the French hood arrived during the late 1520s. With the French hood a lady could more easily show her hair at her brow.[12] Anne Boleyn advocated the style, always showing part of her hair, which, being dark, complimented her alluring eyes.

Tudors loved French romances such as *Gawain and the Green Knight*. Perhaps influenced by these, the heroines courtiers admired most of all were blond. Characters that were evil, such as Morgan La Fay, were generally depicted as dark-haired. The medievals and Tudors even used words such as 'clarissant' and 'lienor' to describe beautiful hair. Recipes existed aimed to turn hair golden such as: 'Apply overnight a paste of ashes boiled for half a day in vinegar.' The concoction acted like a beaching agent. Rhubarb and white wine provided another method to achieve blonder heads.[13] Two of Henry's recorded mistresses were blond, they were Mary Boleyn and Elizabeth Blount. Anne Boleyn may have been dark, but possessed beautiful, luxuriant, very long hair and lovely dark eyes.

\* \* \*

Did men ever dress as women and vice versa? Well, they did. Cross-dressing, dressing up, drag and transvestism, Peter Ackroyd tells us, 'is the survival of an ancient and natural tendency of primitive man and is not a sexual anomaly'.[14] Cross-dressing during the medieval and early Tudor era might simply reflect admiration and affection for the opposite sex. One theory is that man could be so attracted to a woman he wished to become permanently or intermittently identified with the female sex even though Christianity seriously suppressed this particular desire, at least in theory.

Yet herein lies yet another religious contradiction. On a particular medieval feast day celebrated in Northern Europe down through the ages into our own era, The Feast of Fools, initially held in Northern France and later more widely, participants would elect a false bishop or pope and parody ecclesiastical rites, dressed in female clothing. The occasion was originally connected to medieval drama, and earlier was celebrated on the first of January, the Roman Kalends of January, the Feast of Circumcision. On this day, traditionally, high and low clergy swapped places in order to reflect humility. It was an example of one occasion when laymen and clergy dressed as women, howled through the church aisles and made a farcical nonsense of the liturgy.

Transvestism of this kind was severely condemned by Church authorities since it derived from ecstatic cults and was pervaded by the notion of chaos. Festive societies known as Abbeys of Misrule existed in France and Italy, and they were transvestite in character. The societies represented an alternative to conventional sexual social behaviour. Dressing up was part of their festive agenda. Such dressing up was only socially acceptable when it *could* be controlled at annual festivals where licensed anarchy was perceived as a useful escape valve for otherwise dangerous tensions in the form of secret existent transvestite prostitution. The tradition was a marginally social function, especially in societies where women were not readily available for sexual purposes and monasticism was such a situation.

The Feast of Fools finally became secularised during the sixteenth century. At the Epiphany Feast, Twelfth Night, celebrated on 6 January, a Lord of Misrule's election contained transvestite aspects. The Lord of Misrule originally chose twenty *lustiguts* to serve him, all of them dressed in female clothing. In England, the Lord of Misrule was appointed by a popular lot, or by finding a bean hidden in a celebratory cake; his task was to oversee the festival of fools at Christmastide. Twelfth Night often included drunkenness and wild partying. John Stow in his Survey of London [1603] wrote:

> In the feaste of Christmas, there was in the kings house, wheresoeuer he was lodged, a Lord of Misrule, or Maister of merry disports, and the like had yee in the house of euery noble man, of honour, or good worshippe, were he spirituall or temporall. Among the which the Mayor of London, and eyther of the shiriffes had their seuerall Lordes of Misrule, euer contending without quarrel or offence, who should make the rarest pastimes to delight the Beholders ... In all which space there were fine and subtle disguisings, Maskes and Mummeries, with playing at Cardes for Counters, Nayles and pointes in every house, more for pastimes than for gain.[15]

The Christmas tradition of the Lord of Misrule remained in place throughout the Tudor era but was banned by Puritan rule during the seventeenth century and was never revived after the Restoration. Other interesting snippets about cross-dressing activity exist for this period. Henry III of France (1551–1589), for instance, is reported to have dressed as an Amazon, and encouraged his male courtiers to do likewise.

Women who dressed in men's clothing were on occasion monks or hermits. During the medieval period the cult of the bearded woman saint was part of medieval folklore in Western Europe. Female cross-dressing was associated with sexual deviancy. To the medieval and early

Tudor person, women's transvestism suggested a syr
woman's femininity and therefore the medieval belief
traditional male and female roles. The medieval and
sorcery emphasised how dangerous female cross-dres
any woman practising unconformity in this way was ~~~p~~~~~~ ~~ ~~~~~~y
and witchcraft.[16]

Cross-dressing occurred in drama. No actresses were permitted during
the Tudor era (except in court pageants, of which there were many) and
techniques were developed during the Tudor period to encourage actors
to display the skilful natural deployment of feminine characteristics. By
the mid sixteenth century women's theatrical roles were complex enough
to demand special skills of speech as well as dress. Creating the illusion of
imitating women meant child actors became popular.[17] During the second
half of the century, the Elizabethan era, 'Boys' Companies' dominated the
English theatre. They relied on expressive talents and realistic costuming
for the creation of the very best dramatic effects. Such techniques had
their genesis during the time of Henry VIII when plays were performed
at court. Elizabethan playhouses came later.

Court cases existed during the sixteenth century which were levelled
against cross-dressers. Mostly they were brought on the basis of breaking
sumptuary laws, the laws prescribing attire to be worn by people of
different social ranks. Male and female cross-dressing posed a threat to
established power relations defined by sumptuary laws. Cross-dressers
could, using this excuse, be prosecuted by authorities.[18] Female to male
cross-dressing remained a sign of unruliness, and an unruly woman was
perceived as dangerous.

It is possible to see references to cross-dressing in Tudor literature
other than in the later plays by William Shakespeare since cross-dressing
and more advanced attitudes towards women exist in sixteenth-century
Utopian literature. Plato's *Republic*, which influenced Sir Thomas
More's idealistic text, *Utopia*, was renowned for its controversial views
on women's roles. More's book includes a patriarchal order and the novel
idea of an examination of the potentially betrothed man and woman
by a third party before marriage for their suitability to marry. He also
refers to a more reasonable attitude to divorce than is normal for the
times. Ironically, Sir Thomas More, who objected to Henry VIII's
divorce, died because he would not agree the *Act of Succession*, naming

cess Elizabeth as first in the line of succession, at least until Henry nd Anne Boleyn had a male child. More had opposed Henry's divorce with Catherine of Aragon and while he believed in Church reform, he perceived Protestants as heretics. They denied transubstantiation, the notion of the miraculous change from communion wine to blood and communion bread into the body of Christ, which was unacceptable to Thomas More and to Henry VIII.

In a text called *Mundus Alter et Idem*, a satirical Utopian fantasy attributed to Joseph Hall (1574–1660), there exists a Hermaphrodite island where everything possesses a double kind. Dress code on this literary island became an outward sign of dual-sexed nature. Men's wit and a woman's craft merge as a perfect union of opposites. Conventional sexual distinctions govern the direction of the dual cross-dressing in the book. Some people on the fantasy island have mostly manly traits while others are better at those displayed by womankind. The style of dress indicates the dominant sex within the person, as does a selection of characters' names – names defined as Mary-Peter or Peter-Alice and so on. In this fantasy world gender differences result from social and cultural practise.[19] *Mundus Alter et Idem* was written a little later than the period mostly covered in this book, but it is fascinating that such ideas existed in, at least, fantasy form during the sixteenth century.

A minority of Tudors enjoyed cross-dressing, either for plays and pageants or as a secret activity. Courtiers always loved dressing up to attract or impress both sexes, just as we do in our modern society. It does not, by any stretch of the imagination, suggest sexual liberation. In fact, Renaissance thought considered women as *the second sex*. Women were, for centuries to come, usually considered weaker than men physiologically and biologically.

### Tudor Dance and Music

Katherine Howard, King Henry VIII's fifth queen, loved to dance and was so adept that Anne of Cleves asked her for dance lessons during the short period when Katherine was a maid of honour at Anne's court. Henry VIII, when he was younger, was also a lover of music and dance, a desirable skill at court. Katherine Howard first caught his eye, it is said, while dancing for him, an occasion set up by her Uncle Thomas, the Earl of Norfolk. She had, as was revealed later, permitted her dancing master privileges with her person when she was barely into her teens and living with her grandmother, the earl's mother.

Dancing was one way for the sexes to meet each other; not surprising then that it has always been so popular throughout history. Young men wishing to socialise with prospective wives could easily do so through dancing. It allowed them to show off their grace and good health and to get physically close to someone of the opposite sex in a way unpermitted otherwise.[1]

Whether poor or wealthy, most people enjoyed music and dance. Dancing steps varied between upper and lower classes. Tudor court dances were complicated and stately. They possessed intricate steps favoured by the nobility and wealthy whereas in towns and villages medieval English country dances were simpler and great traditional favourites, similar to country dances today.

Court dances were performed as couples. The dance named the Volt was the most suggestive of courtly dances and allowed couples to closely embrace. Other popular dances with the wealthy were the Pavan, Gilliard, the Gavotte, and the Almain, or variations of these. Tudor courtiers travelled abroad and returned with new dances from Spain, Italy and France, and since such dances all had to be learned, dancing masters were popular and easily gained employment. Famous dancing masters of the Age were Thoinot Arbeau (1520–1595), Fabritto Caroso (1536–1605) and Caesare Negri (1535–1604). These instructors produced manuals that were printed and sold throughout Europe. The new manuals included innovative steps such as walking steps, cutting steps, sliding, stamping, leaping, jumping and hopping. In a dance such as the stately Pavane the woman's hand rested on top of the man's hand when partnered, not clasped tightly at all. This symbolically represented her ability to escape in flight if her partner was too fresh. There's a rather amusing and delightful YouTube video with Danny Dyer showing this (and, as an aside, selecting his codpiece for his venture into the ways of the Tudor Court). Dance manuals emphasised the social role of dance. Arbeau wrote that dancing was practised to reveal whether lovers were in good health and limb, after which they were permitted to kiss their mistresses in order that they may touch one another to ascertain 'if they are shapely or omit an unpleasant ordour of bad meat.'[2]

Dancing was condemned in certain circles as encouraging immorality because of the link between dance and love. Most courtiers could point to how the Bible approved dancing (King David danced before the Ark). Others said it upheld the intellectual humanist theory that the harmonious movements of dance echoed the movements of the stars. Men and women dancing together represented perfect harmony since men's fiercer natures were tempered and balanced by a woman's gentler virtues. Women, argued Arbeau, were not permitted the same freedom as men and therefore their opportunities for exercise were limited. It was acceptable for women to partner another woman. Anne of Cleves danced with Queen Katherine Howard at the Christmas festivities of 1540 when King Henry retired early. It was also important not to show off or draw attention to one's dancing skills according to *The Book of the Courtier* by Castiglione. Dancing was connected to courtship and good dancing illuminated good breeding, so dancing masters taught deportment and etiquette as well as the moves to the dances listed below.

**The Pavane** was a stately processional dance. Tudor couples paraded around the hall lightly touching fingers. Pavane means 'peacock' so the dance title derives from the sight of women's gowns trailing over the floor like a peacock's tail. The aim of the Pavane was to demonstrate dancing skills, but in addition to show off fine clothes to the best advantage. The dance was made up of a pattern of five steps. Another name used for the Pavane was Cinque Pas. It was popular for court masques.

**The Galliard** was a lively dance that originated in the fifteenth century. It followed and complimented The Pavane. A similar dance that originated in France was the Satarella.

**The Almain** was an important dance accompanied by keyboard instruments and lute music. It had a 'double-knocking' upbeat. Dancers formed a line of couples who took hands and walked the length of the room, walking three steps then balancing on one foot. Occasionally, they used three springing steps and a hop. Couples could also hold one forearm and turn around to each other to the left or right. It could be a close dance and maybe both suggestive and lively.

**The Volt** was another suggestive dance when women were lifted high by a male partner.

**The Courant** was a slow moving, elegant dance which came from France.

**The Canary** was a Spanish dance that was strange and fantastic, also popular in France. It was known as a lively wooing dance with rapid heel-to-toe stamps. It was occasionally known as 'frogs legs' because it was energetic and featured jumps, stamping of feet and violent movement. The musical accompaniment had syncopated rhythms.

**The Gavotte** was basically an amusing kissing game associated with love. It originated as a French folk dance from the south east and was the last of a Suite of Branles. The kissing was later replaced by the presentation of flowers. The Gavotte was stately with a lifting step. It was danced in a line or circle to music in double time with little springs and steps borrowed from the Galliard. Carly Simon's song *You're so Vain* contains the line, 'You had one eye on the mirror as you watched yourself gavotte.' So much for not showing off. Tudors did try to create an impression while dancing.[3]

\* \* \*

Love was a theme that permeated Tudor dance. Many court dances mixed a variety of steps based on the theme of love. The ups and downs of a courtly love affair were represented by movements with complicated floor patterns that were committed to memory. A good performance meant an impressive courtier. A poor performance suggested just the opposite.

In order to ask a lady to dance a man was expected to remove his hat with his left hand and offer his right hand to lead her out to dance. The right side during the sixteenth century was the side of honour. It was also bad manners to wear gloves while dancing. Ladies were allowed to ask men to dance in a quiet manner and to make it apparent whom they were asking. Moreover it was bad manners for a man to decline an invitation.[4]

Dancing was something everyone could enjoy no matter their social status. Different dances were accompanied by appropriate forms of music. New musical instruments were invented during the sixteenth century.

This opened up new sounds and in turn dance adaptations or new dances to go with the music. Upper-class dancers might dance to the lute, the guitar or the sound of louder instruments like shawns and sackbuts, which were hired to play at weddings. The poor, on the other hand, favoured less expensive, much-loved traditional instruments such as bagpipes and hurdy gurdies, along with pipes and tabours.

A courtier was advised to turn to music to show his knowledge of it in conversation. Tudor monarchs did much to make music fashionable. Instruction manuals appeared and help spread musical education whereas the poor still had to learn by ear. Children of the wealthy were taught to sing from song books. Poor children sang older well-known songs and ballads from memory. Throughout the Tudor century the universal interest in music increased in popularity.[5]

Henry VIII was responsible for music's increased popularity as he was a keen musician himself. During his reign he transformed the royal musical household, in part because his aim was to have the most cultured court in Europe. He employed the best musicians, English and foreign. By 1540 he maintained thirty-seven musicians, and his personal collection of musical instruments contained twenty-six lutes. Henry himself played both the lute and virginals. His father, Henry VII, appropriately employed a Welsh harper, four sackbuts, shawn players and a dozen trumpeters. The Tudor age, consequently, echoed with beautifully romantic music, ballads, song and dance.

Oxford and Cambridge had offered degrees with music since the mid-fifteenth century which mostly focused on musical theory. Music was perceived as a gentlemanly pastime rather than as a serious part of a student's studies. The best secular opportunity for employment for a musician other than court was as a city wait. Waits were essentially watchmen who patrolled cities and played instruments to assure people all was well. By the mid-sixteenth century they were officially municipal musicians who played at civic occasions and were available for private hire. London owned six waits who, from 1548, were allowed two apprentices each. Waits possessed summer and winter livery of blue gowns and red caps. They wore silver chains and a silver badge displaying the arms of the city. The musicians were in great demand for weddings and an important citizen might employ them when impressing a betrothed or even a lover.

The lower classes held dances outdoors, lacking the hall space their upper-class betters would possess in manor houses and castles. May Day was a much-loved holiday in Tudor times. Every village, town or hamlet would possess a maypole, dressed on the first day of May with a variety of colourful ribbons each held by a dancer. The dancers would weave in and out around the maypole until eventually their dancing would create a colourful pattern tied about the maypole. As far back as pagan times the maypole was a symbol of fertility and dancing on May Day aimed at producing a good grain crop and bountiful harvest during the coming year.

Banales, which originated as folk dances, were performed in a number of ways – in couples, round dances and in lines. They are still danced in Brittany to this day. Some were even mime dances, for example copying washerwomen's movements at the tub, or arguing with clients. Another banale mocked hermits greeting each other. Banale dances were social in that as many dancers as wished could join in. The Candlestick Banale was a dance in which dancers passed lighted candles between them.

The poor enthusiastically celebrated feast days and weddings with dance and music and one imagines that much courting went on in villages and towns, particularly during May Day or at the Midsummer Feast of St John, and without doubt during other feast days associated with the many festivals celebrated before the Reformation.

# Chapter 6

# Courtly Romance and Poetry

Prior to the Tudor period *Fabliaux*, short metrical tales which were originally popular in medieval France, were appreciated by all classes. These often bawdy poetic tales were enjoyed at the court of Henry VII in the vernacular as well as by the population in general. *Fabliaux* contained vivid detail and realistic observations. They were comic, coarse and often cynical in their treatment of women. For example, Chaucer's *Miller's Tale*, a short story characterised by jokes and sex, was influenced by the *fabliau* tradition. Older odes written during the twelfth century by Eleanor of Aquitaine's grandfather and others contain crude vulgarities intertwined with eloquent romantic love. In addition to these *fabliaux*, lais (short, romantic poetry), ballads and Chaucer's mix of older medieval tradition, Henry's father, Henry VII, also promoted tales of Arthurian legend. Henry VIII adored them and owned copies of Arthurian chivalric stories.

The concept of courtly love was an integral part of chivalric poetry. Chivalric literature associated with Arthurian legends, the siege of Troy, and all works by Geoffrey Chaucer was central to the cultural life of the early Tudor court. Of all verse, Chivalric poetry was the most popular, read and recited during the early Tudor Age in court circles. Surrey's poetry evokes a romantic, aristocratic medieval world of chivalry and tournaments. Chivalric artifices occupied the nobility in their pursuit of entertainment. As Henry VIII wrote in his song *Pastime with Good Company*, youth must have some dalliance:

> Of good or ill some pastance.
> Company methinks then best
> All thoughts and fancies to digest
> For idleness
> Is chief mistress
> Of vices all.

Hunting, dancing, music, poetry, good conversation and the game of courtly love was the preferred activity for the Tudor gentleman when he was not engaged in training in the pseudo-war of the tournament or in actual war.[1]

Courtly love was the domestic arm of chivalry. Since the twelfth century, when writers were earnest about chivalric code, courtly love poetry and the pursuit of courtly love had morphed into ornamental pastiche. Geoffrey Chaucer was England's Virgil. During the first three and a half decades of the Tudor era he remained England's pre-eminent poet. With Chaucer's success and the emergence of the age of print, English was considered at the Tudor court a perfect language to convey story and verse.[2]

By the 1520s a new form of introspective poetry was emerging. Initially this new poetry was written by poets associated with Henry VIII's Renaissance court. In this chapter I discuss two Renaissance poets and how a manuscript anonymously written by many youthful hands at Anne Boleyn's court was prompted by personal matters and fashionably penned in an evolving sonnet form.

*   *   *

Poetry was beginning to change in form and content. By the second and third decades of the sixteenth century Renaissance poetry began to reflect a poet's personal inner feelings with a larger degree of sincerity rather than playing with courtship as reflected within the game of courtly love. Poetry was using new forms to express feelings of love and sexuality.

The Petrarchan sonnet had arrived. This was an innovative form assumed to have initially been brought to England from Italy by the courtly scribe Sir Thomas Wyatt.[3] Humanists of the era had quested for a meter that would capture in the vernacular the flavour of unrhymed verse and this new sonnet form provided something new and thrilling. Sixteenth-century blank verse traditionally used a ten syllable meter without the security of rhyme. Surrey, for example, favoured order and proportion in poetry and he loved the new form's discipline. Using it, his poetry could feel stately, reflecting his somewhat elitist aristocratic leaning.

The Earl of Surrey, Henry Howard, heir to the infamous third Duke of Norfolk, was a true English Renaissance man. He was one of the famous court poets of the Henrician Age. Surrey was a humanist, interested in Greek and Roman learning and in debating texts connected to antiquity. He saw cultural innovation as a way to give a new lustre to the noble class itself, not just to poetry. His love poems are tightly expressed and precise, lyrical and romantic both.

> Love that doth reign and live within my thought
> And built his seat within my captive breast
> Clad in the arms wherein me he fought
> Oft in my face he doth his banner rest
> But she that taught me love and suffer pain
> My doubtful hope and eke my hot desire.[4]

By the mid-1530s, for Surrey, the game of courtly love became real, touching him with consequences that belong to the world of chivalric legends. Events played out within his family led to scarily tangible consequences associated with forbidden love. This particular story of romantic love is worth recounting here. Surrey, himself, wrote verses connected to a family scandal. These were later inserted into a manuscript passed amongst a clique of courtiers who dabbled in poetry. [5] The text containing the lines, possibly written by Surrey, is known as *the Devonshire Manuscript*. Today it is held in The British Library.

Firstly, an explanation of the origins of *the Devonshire Manuscript*. This was a volume of poems associated with Surrey's sister, Mary Howard, whose initials appear on the original binding. Queen Anne's waiting woman, Madge Shelton, was also involved, as was the King's twenty-year-old niece, Margaret Douglas. There is actually a joint inscription to Margaret Douglas and Mary Shelton within the book.[6] Poems in this work were scribed by at least twenty different hands. It was passed around Anne Boleyn's close group, not dissimilar to the way in which we use social media today. The verses in the manuscript invited dialogue through which a group of courtly persons wrote to, for and about each, written in stylised terms.

The courtiers contributing to *the Devonshire Manuscript* had access to love poetry by Thomas Wyatt who used sonnet form in his verse and it was Wyatt's sonnets rather than the popular courtly verse of Geoffrey

Chaucer that influenced the manuscript verses. Since the book was circulated with blank leaves, recipients conversed with each other using responses, by adding lines and by changing lines. A sentiment expressed in one lyric was answered in another. It returned at intervals to Mary Shelton herself, who would alter any misogynistic lines to pro-feminist ones. Metaphors of courtly love poetry included imprisonment, dying, suffering, accusation, betrayal, concealment, and the notion that one could really die for love.[7]

Henry Howard alludes to a relationship between young Thomas Howard, a step-brother of Thomas Howard, third Duke of Norfolk, and Lady Margaret Douglas, the King's niece. He is thought to have written the lines, 'In playful fable each beste can chose his feare.' As a degree of proof, Surrey's name even appears in the manuscript. The lines refer to the romance and its unfortunate consequences for the younger Thomas Howard who had made a private contract of marriage with Margaret Douglas, daughter of King Henry's sister, Margaret of Scotland, and therefore a young lady close to the succession. Their situation, a forbidden romance, became one of *the Devonshire Manuscript's* focal points. The love story is a literal illustration of how the tropes of courtly love were evolving and merging with the new sonnet form.

Anne Boleyn disapproved of the clandestine relationship between Howard and Douglas, and, since they were part of Queen Anne's circle, the couple met secretly. An early poem in the manuscript charting the romance says for example:

> Take heed betime lest ye be spied
> Your loving eyes ye cannot hide
> At last the truth will sure be tried
> Therefore take heed.
> For some there be of crafty kind,
> Though you show no part of your mind,
> Surely their eyes cannot be blind.
> Therefore take heed.[8]

*Some* is thought to refer to Anne Boleyn, a warning to be careful to avoid the Queen's sharp eyes. The likelihood is that the couple would keep a look out until Queen Anne was not in her chambers and meet clandestinely. When their secret marriage *per verba de presenti* occurred, only two persons were party to the secret wedding, Lady Williams and Hastings, a servant to Thomas's mother.

The situation imploded two months after the execution of Anne Boleyn. The pair were arrested because Margaret's place in the succession had catapulted her into enormous political importance. That July, two months after Anne's execution, Eustace Chapuys, the Spanish ambassador, wrote in dispatches following the arrest of Margaret Douglas that a person of *Blood Royal* was also to die, but added that for the present this person was pardoned her life considering that sexual intercourse had not taken place. Had it done so she 'deserved pardon seeing the number of domestic examples she has seen.'[9] Perhaps this comment was Chapuys's personal dig at the perceived raciness of Anne Boleyn's court. The Spanish ambassador had no liking for Queen Anne.

Margaret's relationship with Thomas Howard had unfortunately brought him into the realm of dynastic politics. Their relationship and secret marriage became perceived as a threat to the succession, one that Henry VIII was not prepared to tolerate. His own niece's marriage was within his royal prerogative. England's revised Treason Act during the 1530s meant that such dalliance was not at all sanctioned, and worse it was regarded as treason.[10] An Act of Attainder on 18 July 1536 affected both Margaret Douglas and Thomas Howard, causing them to be placed in the Tower (the Act forbade the marriage of any member of the king's family without the king's permission).[11] While imprisoned in the Tower, the romantic couple continued to write courtly poems which were later slipped into the manuscript. It is impossible to prove conclusively that Thomas wrote the prison poems later placed in the collection because there is a lack of attested example of his handwriting. His authorship cannot be disproved either. Margaret was treated leniently. After she fell ill, she was moved to Syon Abbey under the supervision of Syon's abbess and she was released on 27 October 1537. Thomas, under sentence of death, was spared execution but he remained in the Tower, where he died on 31 October 1537.[12]

Many poems contained within this manuscript refer to the plight of imprisoned lovers who are unjustly torn apart. They are poignant love poems. Here are two examples:

> For term of life thy gift you have
> Thus now adieu my own sweet wife
> From TH which no light doth crave
> But you the stay of all my life.

Assuming he is the poet, Howard wrote the following lines in prison:

> Alas that men can be so revengeful
> To order me so cruelly
> Of right they should themselves repent
> If they regard their honesty.

Paranoia and surveillance were a primary component of King Henry's court. Courtiers involved in the writings in *the Devonshire Manuscript* were just as self-involved as the youth of any generation since can be. Their poems were a vehicle for the most interesting of youthful preoccupations – their own personal social dramas and their own coded and secret messages as inscribed in lyrics. The manuscript in itself was as enthralling during the 1530s for the clique involved with its creation as it grips hold of our imagination today. It is a captivating glimpse into the youthful aspect of Henrician courtly society.

\* \* \*

While the traditional courtly lyric had been a late medieval tradition, private concerns of sexuality, love and relations between the sexes by the 1520s clearly begin to emerge. The manuscript is only one example where poems pose questions about relations between the sexes at the Tudor court.

The Reformation brought spiritual equality but certainly not autonomy for women in society. For those men who desired same-sex relationships or were bisexual, sodomy became a capital offence in 1533. With the advent of Protestant thought, sexual conduct was even further regularised, not enlightened. Friendships expressed through poetry could assume great intensity in contrast to what was actually expected or permitted by Tudor status quo. In *the Devonshire* poems one discovers complaints such as the lament of the seduced woman, a genre that later appealed to Shakespeare, whose own poem *A Lover's Complaint* reflects poetic debates dating from the 1520s and 1530s.

Was Renaissance man sexist? Was Renaissance woman allowed to speak? 'Yes' to the former as we understand sexism today and 'no' to the second, generally speaking. There was a long way to go, centuries in fact, before women's voices could be heard and recognised. In Sir Thomas Wyatt's poetry, there is an illusion of freedom in love as he debates the nature of romantic and physical love. Nowhere in Wyatt's poetry is there a greater sense of debate about the changing nature of love poetry during the Tudor era than in his poem *They Flee from Me*. Rather having to be wooed and won by the services of lovers women are 'wyld' creatures and love is 'sought, caught and kissed'.[13]

Wyatt was a court poet, yet he was not a courtly entertainer who wanted to write festival poems to keep the court happy celebrating occasions such as May Day. Wyatt tried to reconcile the courtly way of life with the deeper conventions reflecting the game of love. He wrote about suffering lovers. He used familiar devices such as hawking to present erotic suggestions. In his poem *They Flee from Me* women are not depicted as passive:

> They fly from me that some time did me seek
> With naked foot stalking in my chamber
> I have seen them gentle, tame and meek
> That now are wyld and do not remember
> That sometimes they put themselves in danger
> To take bread at my hand and now they range
> Busily seeking with continual change.[14]

This poem represents a feeling more real than the personified fear of shame, particularly a woman's shame, as is usually evident in fourteenth and fifteenth century writing. There is a suggestion in the poem that the courtly game of love is inadequate. While lovers seek real love, they are unable to satisfy their own needs because of long-held conventions. A sense of emotional anguish penetrates the above scene painted by Wyatt.

*They Flee from Me* is a conventional and unconventional poem, written in what is known as rhyme royal, a poetic form introduced into literature by Geoffrey Chaucer. A failure of communication is reduced to a game of love in which neither wins or loses and therefore must seek to pass the time pleasantly. The emotional price of true love was way too high for a Tudor, as the story of Thomas Howard and Margaret Douglas illustrates. *They Fly from Me* suggests how the human heart at this time cannot reach out to another human heart in this way because of society's expectations. The pretence of courtly love cannot make the heart beat fast. Irrationality, a feature of romantic love is too painful. Love remains a difficult emotional and social maze.

A heightened degree of subjectivity and individuality entered the world of poetry during the 1530s with the transition from courtly love poetry to a more modern intellectual poetry. The legacy of the early Renaissance poets passes forward to Shakespeare, Donne, Marvell and beyond. These poets developed poetry into something so personal it represents their own personal desires. As the Modern Age was born during the sixteenth century, emotion increasingly matters to the new humanist, the Renaissance man.

Wyatt was one of the men arrested at the time of Anne Boleyn's fall in May 1536. Queen Anne's first response on discovering who was held in the Tower with her was 'They may well make pallets now.' It was a clever pun on the word 'ballad'.[15] Wyatt was imprisoned in the Bell Tower, a gracious lodging for prisoners of high status. After his arrest Thomas Cromwell gathered juries together. He commuted any outcome for the poet to honourable detention. Cromwell's friendship with Wyatt's father would never have been the sole reason. It is likely that Wyatt agreed to inform on the accused. What he may have said is not in the Historical Record. Since loyalty to the King was important to adhere to, the unfortunate poet may have had little option but to speak to investigators. Whatever Wyatt said, Thomas Cromwell appears to have paid him £100 for saying it. It could have been connected to the odd details of the accusations against Anne, such as her laughing at the King's verse or making fun of his costuming. Wyatt was an authority on poetry and pageantry. Anne Boleyn, who loved verse and pageantry, may have commented to Wyatt negatively about the King's verse. Her comments could easily have been twisted into serious mockery of Henry.

A sense of self-preservation prevailed amongst courtiers after the executions of Anne Boleyn and the young men accused with her. A last chilling poem in *the Devonshire Manuscript* contains the following lines:

> To counterfeit a merry mood
> In mourning mind I think it best,
> But once in rain I wore a hood
> Well they were wet that bare-headed stood
> But since that cloaks are good for doubt
> The beggars' proverb find I good:
> Better a path than a hall out[16]

'Rain' is a pun on 'reign', and for 'in mourning mind' read 'in mourning wise'. Wyatt was traumatised by his experience in prison at this time and he wrote several poems alluding to his experience. His lines are chilling:

> The bell tower showed me such a sight
> That sticks in my head day and night.[17]

Wyatt observed how lightness left love and how Anne Boleyn, the King's great *amour*, was snatched from earth along with men Wyatt had known most of his life.[19] He emerged from the Tower shocked, sobered and until 1540 and Cromwell's execution, he remained Thomas Cromwell's man.

Wyatt's personal life contains several love stories. In appearance he was over six feet tall and allegedly handsome. He married Elizabeth Brook with whom he had one son, also called Thomas and who led the Wyatt Rebellion during Queen Mary I's reign. Sir Thomas Wyatt wrote ninety-six love poems which appeared posthumously in 1557 in *Tottel's Miscellany*. They included thirty-one sonnets in English. Thomas Wyatt was alleged by many historians to have been in love with Anne Boleyn during the early 1520s. His famous sonnet *Whoso List to Hunt* possibly alludes to Anne's relationship with King Henry:

> Craven in diamonds with letters plain
> There is written her fair neck round about
> Noli me tangere, for Caesar's I am.[18]

A deer mentioned in this poem comes straight out of a previous Petrarchan poem referring to a courtly lady pursued by suitors in ancient times. In the Italian poem *The Lady* is protected from molestation by Caesar's laws of marriage. By 1533, a possible date for this poem,[19] Wyatt knew that Anne Boleyn belonged to an English Caesar.

Wyatt's wife had been unfaithful to him, a huge faux pas in the Tudor era but it occurred. Katharine Parr's sister-in-law also left her husband for a lover. Wyatt had several affairs, acceptable for men but never for women. Katherine Howard unsuccessfully encouraged a reconciliation between Wyatt and his estranged wife. By now Wyatt had a mistress he loved who proceeded to have three children by him. He never returned to his wife. Sir Thomas Wyatt, the greatest early Tudor poet, most remembered for his sonnets and enigmatic love poetry, died during the early 1540s, just as the Henrician Age was drawing towards its evening years.

# Chapter 7

# Noli me tangere, for Caesar's I am

This book cannot omit the most significant and arguably one of the most unfortunate love stories of the Tudor court. Poetry making, as explained in the previous chapter, was a key courtly skill dangerously associated with sexual frustration, wishful thinking and actual sexual liaisons at court. Anne Boleyn's relationship with Henry VIII, her marriage and her queenship is a path well-trodden by writers, as are the accusations of sexual adultery and incest made against her and her brother in May 1536. I shall, therefore, be succinct about this courtly romance.

King Henry VIII wrote verses of his own, but unlike those in *The Devonshire manuscript*, Henry's poems were signed. There is no clever wordplay in Henry's love poems; no brilliant puns as one would discover in Sir Thomas Wyatt's love poems. Nor are there admirable allusions to classical works or perfect structure as appears in the Earl of Surrey's poems. They do not contain hidden messages. Henry's poems, and romantic correspondence with Anne Boleyn, are clumsy, straightforward, earnest and gallant.

He wrote, for example, complaining he had not heard from her, 'you have not been pleased to remember the promise which you made me ... which was that I should hear good news of you.' And in another letter, having heard a report that she has changed her mind about him and will not come to court, 'It seems small return for the great love I bear you, to be kept at a distance from the person and presence of the woman in the world that I value the most ... though this will not distress the mistress as much as the servant. Consider well, my mistress, how greatly my absence from you grieves me; I hope it is not your will that it should be so; but if I heard for certain that you yourself desired it, I could do no more than complain of my ill-fortune, and by degrees abate my great folly.'[1]

No one knows if Anne Boleyn ever loved King Henry. She did not appear to rate his verse-making. Henry's poems were never fresh new compositions but rather lines added to existent poems and songs. The romantic lines he scribed dwindled after his marriage to Anne although he apparently wrote a few impoverished romantic verses to Catherine Parr years later. As Eric Ives wrote about the royal marriage: 'Anne won her way by education, personality and courage.' He also wrote, 'now she had to accept that success as an individual was unimportant against biological success or failure.'[2] Anne was expected to provide England and Henry with a longed-for legitimate son. The days of romantic love were over and, possibly, physical desire had waned too once she was conquered.

Princesses of the blood were raised to see providing an heir as their future. It was expected of them and they understood marriages were contracts designed largely to provide heirs. With Anne Boleyn, King Henry was building a relationship not with a woman who had been sent to him by any diplomatic marriage but one to whom he was sexually and intellectually attracted.[3] Only two other kings since the Norman Conquest married for love and sexual attraction. Some medieval kings *did* end up loving their wives, if not at first. There was an element of romantic love involved initially in the courtship between Joan of Navarre and Henry IV. Edward IV, Henry's grandfather, whom Henry resembled in looks, also married Elizabeth Woodville, a commoner, for love and sexual attraction. This marriage caused enormous problems as the Wars of the Roses drew to a close when Edward V, the boy King, Edward IV's heir, mysteriously disappeared in the Tower of London. It was put out by Woodville's enemies that Edward's sons were illegitimate because his father had been pre-contracted earlier to another courtly lady. The importance of a pre-contract at this time cannot be underestimated even though it took sex to make a marriage a legal one. The argument concerning Elizabeth Woodville's sons was flimsy and convenient.

In the case of Anne Boleyn and Henry VIII there was great romantic emotion involved. They fell in love or, at least, Henry fell in love or lust, or both, with Anne. However, Anne Boleyn did not turn a blind eye, as she was expected to, when Henry's interest later strayed and, even more significantly, she failed to give him a son. Any Boleyn correspondence with Henry referring to their courtship was most likely destroyed after her execution, but some letters famously written from Henry to Anne exist. These prove that Henry genuinely had a huge sexual and emotional passion for Anne. As for Anne, we just don't know her feelings because of the lack of correspondence and writings from the time.

We do know that Anne, for her part, played at courtly love with Henry. She was probably attracted to him because Henry was, after all, the King, attractive, powerful, and, of course, fabulously rich. Anne Boleyn had come to court in March 1522 and, though there were plans for her to marry Piers Butler, it was soon whispered about the court that Anne was King Henry's *amorata*. Henry, meanwhile, was increasingly troubled by his childless marriage, having no heir except for a daughter.

During 1522 Henry was involved with Anne's married sister, Mary. Eric Ives describes Anne as showing up at court looking very haughty and self-confident, 'having all manner of jewels and rich apparel that might be gotten with money.'[4] Soon after her arrival at court Anne became involved with young Harry Percy who was at this time in Cardinal Wolsey's household. The problem was Harry Percy was already betrothed. Since she was a maid of honour to Queen Catherine, Percy hung around the Queen's chambers, clearly entranced by Anne. A secret love grew between Anne and Percy. Many historians believe they intended marriage, although it is unlikely they actually had slept together given how long she made Henry wait. Henry, by now, was very taken with Anne and ordered Wolsey to intervene in the budding romance between Anne and Percy.[5]

Percy was told to back off but he defended his right to choose his own bride. He also upheld the sexy, intelligent Anne's suitability to be his wife. Cardinal Wolsey immediately sent for Percy's father and meantime forbade Percy to see Anne. Henry Percy was given a public dressing down by his father who had hot-footed it to London from his seat in Northumberland, apparently saying, 'Son, thou hast always been a proud, presumptuous, disdainful and unthrifty waster and so hast thou now declared thyself.'[6]

Percy was already betrothed to Mary Talbot. No sex had occurred therefore this betrothal could have been broken, but threats were made to Percy concerning the King's displeasure. Percy was also threatened with disinheritance by his father. Wolsey quickly found a way to invalidate Percy's hand-fasted commitment to Anne Boleyn and she was sent packing home to Hever Castle. Percy was later married, very unhappily, to Mary Talbot. Anne hated Wolsey thereafter and was quoted as saying if it ever lay in her power, she would work Cardinal Wolsey similar displeasure. The experience ruined Henry Percy. His marriage to Mary Talbot floundered and his health collapsed.

Later, as marriage between Henry and Anne approached, Henry Percy swore before the Archbishop of Canterbury there had been no pre-contract between himself and Anne Boleyn. He was, however, reported by the Spanish ambassador, Chapuys, to have appeared very frightened at the time of Anne's fall. The Boleyn-Butler marriage proposal had also floundered. The dispensation Henry sought from the Pope to allow him to marry when free to do so sought to cover any problems attributed to his intended bride such as any pre-contracted marriage with some other person, provided she had not consummated it.

The development of the relationship between Anne and Henry is chronicled in the love letters written by Henry to her. In the first three letters Henry tries to follow the conventions of courtly romance and turning it into a more serious procedure. He famously sent her a buck that he had killed on the previous evening. He chides her for not keeping her promise to write to him and not replying to his earlier letter. The next Letter from Henry to Anne is very serious. Henry is utterly smitten. Even so, she refused to sleep with him and stayed away from court until Henry decided he could not live without her. A third love letter from the King shows how Henry is confused by his continued feelings for Anne. He says he had been a whole year 'struck with the dart of love'. He was not assured of failure nor was he sure of finding a place in her heart but he absolutely wanted a straight answer from her.

For the reader interested in exploring these letters further, I recommend the late Eric Ives' biography of Anne Boleyn. The following four letters showed the relationship between Henry and Anne moving forward in a very serious direction. Now Anne would send him love tokens, as Tudors were wont to do during a courtship. For instance, she sent him a ship with a woman on board with a pendant diamond. The ship symbolised protection, just as did the ark Noah had during the flood. The diamond referred to the well-known romance *Roman de la Rose* which spoke of a 'heart as hard as diamond, steadfast and nothing pliant.'[7] Anne Boleyn was clearly saying yes to Henry's courtship, yet she still refused to sleep with the King who was dying for her, had admired her pretty duckets (breasts) and hoped to kiss them soon. It would seem she allowed him a few sexual favours but not full sexual intercourse.

After he received the ship pendant Henry sent her 'my picture set in a bracelet', a trinket for Anne to remember him by. We do not know what they actually said to each other, or even if Anne suspected that the Aragon marriage was so vulnerable. It is impossible to know if Henry, at first, shared with Anne his concern for the succession. Anne's resistance to sexual relations with him does appear a calculated gamble on her part. She may not have ever wanted to be a discarded royal mistress like her sister, Mary. Long engagements were not the Tudor way. It was likely that by 1527 they hoped to marry within months. Sexual frustration would be over. By this date, only sexual intercourse was lacking to make their relationship a lawful marriage, provided no impediment existed.

Letters from Henry to Anne during 1538 reveal how important the divorce was for her. The marriage went ahead in 1532 and the birth of Elizabeth was followed by several miscarriages which all contributed to her downfall. The Tudor court was inclined to divide into factions and when the centre of all that matters is the King's will *everyone* wanted to gain his favour. Third parties operated efficiently between clients and nobles in favour in return for reward, all to get a person closer to Henry's star. If it was possible for the daughter of a mere English gentlewoman to become queen, this also opened a new way to favour. The Seymour family of Wolf Hall quickly noticed how well the Boleyns had done. They had an available daughter, the mild and malleable Jane, who was a lady-in-waiting to Queen Anne. If Jane could replace Anne the Seymour family could follow in her wake. They coached Jane to place a precious price on her virginity, to tell the King how much people loathed his marriage and how people doubted its validity.

Henry was vulnerable to pressure. Equally, his will was final and factions did not always get their way. However, the Seymours played a long and clever game. By 1535 Jane was the King's focus of chivalry. Anne had already made enemies and was making new ones. Unfortunately for her, one of these was her previous ally Thomas Cromwell and it was Cromwell who finally brought her down with allegations of sexual impropriety.

Early in 1536 Anne and Cromwell quarrelled over the distribution of monastic lands. Queen Anne insulted the King's minister when she had her almoner, John Skip, deliver a sermon based on John 8:36 condemning a Biblical king's advisor and which took a swipe at the

Crown's preoccupation with money, and overtly at the King's rising interest in Jane Seymour. Henry desperately wanted a son. By 1536, after a late January miscarriage on Anne's part, his attentions now seriously strayed in the direction of Jane Seymour.[8]

The well-documented coup engineered by Cromwell followed and Anne, who once had been the recipient of Henry's ardent love letters (which caused a break with the Church of Rome), quickly fell from grace. It was a tragic end to a royal romance and marriage. Anne Boleyn was accused of sexual relations with her musician, Smeaton, who crumbled under questioning at Cromwell's rural residence once he was tortured. Anne was accused of adultery with Henry Norris, an influential man at court and Henry's most intimate body servant and closest friend. Frances Weston, Sir William Brereton and her brother George were all accused of sexual relations with her. These men, except for perhaps Smeaton, were the flower of King Henry's Renaissance court. All except Smeaton denied the charges on their honour. Further arrests included Sir Thomas Wyatt who, in the end, was not accused of adultery with Anne. What Cromwell invented and conspired appears close to imaginative nonsense based on the popular trope of romance poetry where a high lady is taken in adultery.[9]

\*     \*     \*

An interesting question arising from Henry's relations with wives and lovers remains pertinent to this day. Did Henry VIII have sexual problems? He had plenty of sexual relationships and at least two mistresses but only four of the eight women seriously involved with Henry ever conceived children. The last was Jane Seymour in 1537 when Henry was forty-five. Only three pregnancies produced healthy children – Catherine of Aragon, Elizabeth Blount and Anne Boleyn each bore Henry a child who survived childhood. This suggests Henry, not his wives, was at fault. Venereal disease was not thought to be to blame since Henry was never treated for syphilis (his leg ulcer was caused by a fall in the tiltyard).

Henry may have been partially impotent. His divorce from Anne of Cleves was on the grounds of sexual incapacity because he claimed he lacked will and power to consummate the marriage. He had slept with her for months but blamed the absence of sex on his German wife's lack of attractiveness and her unpleasant bodily smell. Henry thought himself very able to complete the act, just not with Anne of Cleves.

At Anne Boleyn's trial, George, her brother, was asked whether Anne ever told his wife, Jane Boleyn, that the king was incapable of sexual intercourse, implying Henry was unable to attain or sustain an erection. A note was handed to George who was ordered to nod or shake his head in response. George Boleyn read it aloud, a move which certainly sealed his fate.[9] He caused a sensation in the court room with his response. Since Anne had conceived four times in three years, it was unlikely, he reported, Anne ever said such a thing. George refused to answer when asked if he had ever expressed doubts that Elizabeth was Henry's child because he might have incriminated himself had he done so.

King Henry associated virility with having children. After a fall in the tiltyard at Greenwich the previous January had knocked Henry unconscious for two hours, Anne miscarried some days later. The child had the appearance of a male, although the foetus's sex may have been guesswork. A deformed foetus story appeared forty years later and can be dismissed as an attempt by Catholic writers to portray Anne as a 'miss-shaped monster'. In the sixteenth century a superstition prevailed that deformity in a baby was a sign of sexual misbehaviour by a parent. The premature foetus and miscarriage, or any strangeness about the foetus could not possibly be the King's fault.[10] This unfortunate miscarriage provided another excuse to investigate Anne's suggested lovers only three months after her January miscarriage.

Henry's priapic dispositions are well recorded. He had six wives and a number of mistresses but only three living children, four including Henry Fitzroy. A theory by the anthropologist Kyra Kramer and the bio-archaeologist Catrina Banks Whitley, writing in *The Historical Journal*, suggests that Henry's blood group may have been the cause of his lost children and lack of heirs. The theory could also explain Henry's midlife physical and mental deterioration.

These researchers suggest Henry's blood carried the rare Kell antigen – a protein that triggers immune responses – while that of his sexual partners did not. It made them poor reproductive matches. In a first pregnancy a Kell-positive man and a Kell-negative woman can have a healthy Kell-positive baby together. In subsequent pregnancies, however, the antibodies the mother produced during the first pregnancy can cross the placenta and attack a Kell-positive foetus causing a late-term miscarriage, stillbirth or death shortly after birth. Henry's sexual encounters with mistresses and his wives resulted in at least eleven and possibly more than thirteen pregnancies. Six children born to Catherine of Aragon were stillborn or died shortly after birth. The survival of three firstborn children, Henry Fitzroy, Elizabeth, and Edward, is consistent with Kell-positive reproductive patterns. Mary may have survived because she inherited the recessive gene from Henry, making her resistant to Catherine's antibodies. The researchers traced evidence for a Kell antigen back to Henry's maternal great-grandmother, Jacquetta of Luxembourg. The pattern of reproductive failure shows in her male descendants while the females were successfully having children that survive. The Kell phenotype was, therefore, within the royal family. Moreover, the McLeod syndrome, a genetic disorder that only affects Kell-positive individuals, may account for Henry's middle-aged instability and extreme leg pain.[11] Other experts have attributed Henry's apparent mental instability to bone infections and to Lyme disease but the Kell theory offers a fascinating and satisfactory explanation for Henry's problems with producing royal heirs.

\* \* \*

The arrests of Anne Boleyn's alleged lovers in May 1536 took place piecemeal. Henry VIII discovered a dispute between Anne and Norris on 29 April. He was seen at a window in Greenwich Palace with Anne who was holding two-and-a-half-year-old Elizabeth. Some kind of remonstration was occurring between the King and Queen according to witnesses. The catalyst was Mark Smeaton, who after twenty-four hours being questioned at Thomas Cromwell's house in Stepney, confessed to adultery with Queen Anne. On May Day 1536 Henry rode from Greenwich to Westminster with Henry Norris. He challenged Norris, who denied adultery both then and during the trials. Henry VIII thereafter became maudlin. For example, he had an exchange with his illegitimate son, Richmond, saying he and his sister, Mary, owed God a great debt for having escaped the hands of the cursed whore who planned to poison them all. At the same time the Seymour faction, as well as Cromwell, were hard at work. During May Henry was making romantic river trips to visit Jane at Beddington near Croydon where she was lodged.[12] Meanwhile, Anne Boleyn was a prisoner in the Tower.

George Boleyn was detained at Whitehall. He may have, in fact, tried to intercede with Henry for his sister, Anne, but had no opportunity to see the King. Boleyn supporters could not reach Henry, who either kept to the gardens or in his own chambers throughout the three weeks prior to Anne's execution. George was accused of adultery and sleeping with his sister – a hanging offence – and this was presented at his trial as fact. Francis Byron was sent for next. Sir Richard Page and Thomas Wyatt were arrested until after it was all over and then released. Brereton was taken to the Tower and accused of adultery with Anne.

During the time of the arrests and accusations the court was exceptionally fearful, especially the Boleyn family. Anne's own father, The Duke of Wiltshire, condemned his daughter's alleged lovers. Stories flew abroad. Reports from France circulated in London to the effect that Anne was guilty of adultery. An anonymous French poem emerged later telling of a plot by Anne, George and their supporters to poison Henry. Two counsellors accused her of adultery with Brereton, Smeaton, Weston, Norris and her brother George.

The Spanish *Cronica del Rey Enrico* has Anne fall for Smeaton. In this account Anne has a fictitious attendant named Margaret. Margaret conceals the naked Smeaton in the antechamber's sweetmeat cupboard. Her role is to produce him when Anne calls for marmalade. One Thomas Percy, who envies Smeaton, tells Thomas Cromwell of the musician's amorous activities with the Queen. The fictitious Margaret is racked and confesses all. Her *imagined* punishment is burning at night in the Tower of London.[13]

Such absurd stories, along with Anne's babblings after her arrest and her nervous collapse, fuelled absurd accusations and helped condemn her. Ladies-in-waiting were interviewed by Thomas Cromwell and their words were twisted. Jane Rochford famously implicated her husband. Rochford's grounds for her accusation was that he had spent overly long in the Queen's bedchamber one evening while alone with her. Much, too, was made of dancing in Queen Anne's chamber when she was passed from partner to partner during a dancing set. George would lead Anne out in the dance. She apparently kissed her brother on occasion and this was described as a deep kiss. Since she wrote to tell George she was pregnant, her letter was exaggerated into a sinister act. Then there was the accusation thast the King was held up to ridicule, with Anne laughing at his clothes and his verse. This much is true. Anne did probe the emotions of her courtiers and that smacked of over familiarity for a Queen. At every turn she was displaying to Henry that other men found her attractive, and maybe she hoped to make him jealous.

Conveniently at the end, just before her execution, Henry had his marriage to Anne annulled by Archbishop Cranmer. One point alluded to in this annulment was that Henry had not validly married Anne because he had previously enjoyed relations with her sister. Before her death, Anne twice swore on the sacrament before the constable of the Tower that she had never been unfaithful to the King. He passed on her oath to Thomas Cromwell.

\* \* \*

The accounts that emerged in some histories written after Anne Boleyn's death, accusing Anne of witchcraft and having a child with her brother which was born deformed and secretly burned, are refuted by more thorough historians such as Eric Ives. Disappointingly, the nonsense exists in some very popular historical fiction, though, in actuality, there were no such accusations at the time. Anne was rarely in the same place as the accused when the alleged adultery took place. Wise to that problem, the Crown added to each charge the catch-all phrase 'And on divers other days and places, before and after.'[14]

Eric Ives writes about the trial of Anne Boleyn: 'Her sparing and effective answers quietly dominated the court.' From the moment of her arrest Anne had recognised the difficulty of establishing her innocence. She said to Kingston, governor of the Tower of London, 'I can say no more but "nay", without I should open my body,' and also, 'if any man accuse me, I can say, but "nay", and they can bring no witnesses.'

Yet when the time came, her manner did carry conviction. No, she had not been unfaithful. No, she had not promised to marry Norris. No, she had not hoped for the King's death. No, she had not given secret tokens to Norris. She had neither poisoned Katherine nor planned to poison Mary. Yes, she had given money to Francis Weston, but she had done the same to many of the always penurious young courtiers, and so it went on. [15]

Eric Ives also refers to how Charles Wriorthesley, a chronicler, who supported Mary and Katherine, thought Anne made wise and discreet answers. Yet, the peers, even the junior peers, pronounced her, 'Guilty, guilty, guilty.' What a conspiratorial set-up that trial was!

Gossip shared with the court, the embellished lechery, a treasonable conspiracy to procure the King's death, the alleged promise to marry a lover after the King's death, The Treason Act of 1352 which stated that simply imagining the King's death was treason, followed by a judicious sequence of suspicion, investigation, evidence and arrest, all based on lies constructed by Cromwell, destroyed Anne Boleyn and those accused of adultery with her. This must be one of the greatest miscarriages of justice associated with sex and sexuality that occurred during the early decades of the Tudor Age.

### Court Mistresses

Henry VIII famously had affairs. By August 1514 Catherine of Aragon was entering her fourth pregnancy and was, according to the Venetian ambassador, 'pregnant and clad in ash-coloured satin with chains and jewels and on her head a cap of gold.' It was not unusual at this time for a woman to have been pregnant four times and not have a living child. One in five newborn children did not survive. Labours could be long and postpartum infections were common. Medical knowledge concerning obstetrics was basic.[1]

Henry was not promiscuous though he famously flirted with court ladies. One of his early amours was Jane Popincourt, a lady who had been at the French court and was in 1509 appointed to Catherine of Aragon's household. Jane Popincourt was notorious. Her reputation was so bad that Louis XII refused to have her as one of Mary Tudor's ladies when King Louis of France married Mary Tudor, the English king's sister. It is not confirmed anywhere that she had an affair with Henry, but he did, at the time of Catherine's pregnancy, give Jane a payment of £100. She later had a known affair with the Duc de Longueville whose wife was in Paris when the Duc was a hostage at the English court.[2]

The Tudor attitude to extra-marital sex was complex. Celibacy, according to Saint Paul, brought a person closer to God. Equally, the Bible promoted family life. Sex was necessary for health and good sex could benefit the appetite and digestion. Bad sex weakened the body and mind. Too much sex was detrimental to health. A theory around at this time suggested every act of sex shortened a man's life by a day. Pleasure was only a secondary intent;[3] sex was for procreation and wasteful spilling of seed was considered wicked by many churchmen. Henry VIII was discreet about his affairs so we really do not know conclusively when any of them began or ended, and, of course, it was socially acceptable for men to have sex with other women when their wives were pregnant.

At the New Year celebrations held at Greenwich in 1515 Elizabeth (Bessie) Blount, one of Catherine's maids of honour, was the centre of attention at the tender age of fourteen or fifteen. She was golden-haired and blue-eyed and skilled in music and dancing. She was dressed in blue velvet, wearing a gold cap and golden mask. Moreover, she partnered King Henry. Catherine of Aragon was so taken with their dancing she asked them to perform again privately for her in her apartments. Henry was smitten by Bessie and she in return was flattered by her king. Henry was twenty-three at the time. Catherine was pregnant again so the King, conventionally, could take a mistress.

By the time Catherine had lost another child in 1519, Bessie Blount was pregnant. In early 1519 Henry entrusted Wolsey to oversee Bessie's confinement with discretion. Henry determined she would have every comfort. She was moved to the Augustine Priory of St Laurence in Blackmore, Essex. It is estimated by historians that Bessie gave birth to a healthy son in June 1519. Bessie Blount's baby boy was proof to King Henry that Catherine was at fault for the lack of healthy male children in their marriage. Cardinal Wolsey stood as godfather for the boy who was named Henry Fitzroy. It was, however, the end of Henry's affair with Bessie because Henry married off his discarded mistress to George, Lord Tailboys of Kyme in Lincolnshire.

Catherine was reported to 'be beyond the ways of women' by 1523. It was a euphemism for the menopause.[4] She was aged thirty-seven. By 1520 Mary Boleyn was Henry's mistress. At this time the Boleyn family was rising as a result of their political acumen and astute marriages, from relative obscurity as tenant farmers to titled gentry with a courtly presence. Thomas Boleyn married Elizabeth, daughter of the second Duke of Norfolk, and after that Boleyn was placed in the upper echelons of society. They had two daughters, Mary and Anne, and a son, George.

Mary served in the King's sister's household in France during Mary Tudor's short marriage to the aged Louis XII of France. When Louis died Mary Boleyn's service was transferred to Claude, the wife of the new king, Francis I. Mary earned a reputation of having been his mistress. Her father recalled her to England where she was given a place in Catherine of Aragon's household. When, in 1520, Mary Boleyn was married to William Carey, a gentleman of the privy chamber, Henry VIII was a guest at the wedding. Mary accompanied the court to France in June 1520 for the event known to history as The Field of the Cloth of Gold.

When King Henry held a tournament on 2 March 1522 he may have chosen Mary to be his lady. On this occasion Henry rode a horse decked with silver caparisons, embroidered with a wounded heart and with the motto 'Elle mon Coeur a navera' (she has wounded my heart). Later, Mary Boleyn took part in a masque, the attack on the Chateau Vert, when ladies were clad in white satin gowns and hats of gold encrusted in gems, and embroidered with their names. Mary was 'Kindness' and Anne, her sister, recently returned from France, appeared as 'Perseverance' (which was, as events revealed later, quite appropriate).

By 1523 Henry's affair with Mary was underway and at this time she gave birth to her first child, Catherine. Catherine was acknowledged unofficially as Henry's daughter rather than William Carey's child. It was at this time that Carey received generous land grants from King Henry, possibly as compensation. Henry Carey was born in March 1526. By this date Mary's affair with Henry was over and Henry Carey was probably William's son. Catherine of Aragon ignored her husband's affairs and focused on her daughter Mary's education. She commissioned Luis Vives to write *The Education of a Christian Woman* in which he advocated that a woman should serve as her husband's companion, 'which was vital to the state'.[5]

For ten years Henry's desire for Anne Boleyn dominated his heart and politics. He told his wife, Catherine, in June 1527 that he doubted the validity of their marriage. By 1528 he wanted his marriage to Catherine annulled. He confided to the papal legate, Cardinal Campeggio, that he had not had sex with Catherine for two years although they shared a bed regularly to keep up appearances. It may be that at this time Henry bedded other women secretly, probably those of a lower class than courtly ladies. He withdrew from court life and passed his leisure time in private.

In August 1533, as Anne Boleyn prepared to enter confinement, there were rumours of a secret liaison between Henry and a beautiful woman. Chapuys remarked, 'The King's affection for her [Anne] is less than it was.' He also wrote, 'He now shows himself in love with another lady and many nobles are assisting him in the affair.' Anne was not as willing as Catherine to turn a blind eye to Henry's dalliances. She was, according to Chapuys, 'very jealous of the King and not without legitimate cause.' When Anne confronted Henry she was told to 'shut her eyes and endure,' as more 'worthy persons had done'.[6]

As Elizabeth was weaned, aged two, Anne was again pregnant and Henry sought diversion again. In February 1535 Chapuys reported that Mary Shelton was enjoying Henry's favour.[7] Mary Shelton was Anne Boleyn's cousin and a lady-in-waiting. The affair lasted approximately six months. During the summer progress of 1535 Henry paid a visit to Wolf Hall, the home of the Seymour family, in Savernake Forest, close to Marlborough in Wiltshire. The Seymours were gentry rather than noble although they boosted an ancient lineage. The Seymour sons, Edward and Thomas, were rising at court. Henry's mission was to woo Jane, their sister. Jane, in contrast to Anne Boleyn, was quiet, pale-skinned and in her mid-twenties. Henry discreetly courted her. Chapuys, famously, could not see what Henry saw her, but wrote that she was 'the most virtuous lady and veriest gentlewoman that liveth.' Chapuys, however, referred to Anne as a 'thin, old and vicious hack.'[8] Anne enticed Henry back to her bed and fell pregnant again. In private, Henry shrank from Anne, but she was pleased, she was pregnant. Unfortunately, though, she miscarried. Jane, meantime, refused to sleep with Henry and so the pair played a courtship game. By 1536, when Thomas Cromwell and Anne became bitter enemies, Cromwell devised his plot to facilitate a new marriage for Henry using Anne's naturally flirtatious nature to destroy her.

During his short marriage to Jane Seymour King Henry appears to have remained faithful. After the birth of Edward and Jane's subsequent death, he became a doting father to his children. Apparently, he had 'a little box of crimson satin with shirts and other things for young children.' It is not known whether these were keepsakes for Elizabeth, Mary and Edward or belonged to the other short-lived babies as well. There is no evidence of scandal touching Henry following Jane's death and none of his three subsequent marriages provided a fourth royal child.

# Chapter 8

# A Visit to a Brothel and Illicit Sex Issues

Never mind royal mistresses and court indulgence in illicit sex, sixteenth- and seventeenth-century theologians maintained their usual attitude of suspicion towards sex and sexuality. Matrimonial chastity remained all important, particularly for women. The Protestant view of 'holy matrimony' was one of shared comfort as well as satisfying sexual desire and procreating legitimate children. Matrimonial chastity meant the moderation of sexual passion. A husband was expected to give his wife enough satisfaction to stop her seeking consolation in other places but not enough to arouse her libido sufficiently to encourage her into extra-marital adventures. Sensuality, lust of the flesh, was usually deemed evil.[1]

Even so, during the early modern period ordinary English attitudes to sensuality were probably freer than in many other parts of Europe. Foreign visitors to England from the late fifteenth century to the eighteenth century noted how persons of different sexes greeted each other with a kiss on the lips. The scholar Erasmus found it an attractive custom: 'Wherever you come, you are received with a kiss by all; when you take your leave, you are dismissed with kisses; you return, kisses are repeated. They come to visit you, kisses again; they leave you, you kiss them all around. Should they meet you anywhere, kisses in abundance; wherever you move, there is nothing but kisses.'[2]

Tudor society had double standards, however. Any sexual positions other than the missionary position with the man on top and woman beneath were rejected as other positions might incite lust. Any approach from behind was condemned because it suggested man was imitating the behaviour of animals. Any position with the woman on top was frowned upon as it inverted sex roles making the woman the dominant partner. Also, the Tudors believed, it reduced the possibility of conception. Use of unnatural orifices such as the mouth or anus and contraceptive notions such as *coitus interruptus* or the newly invented Venus glove (a crude early condom) was forbidden.[3]

These rules were most likely bent in the stews, the name given to brothels of the time. As Kate Lister writes, 'Selling sex is not the oldest profession in the world but sex might be the oldest currency.'[4] Sex has always been traded and attitudes to selling sex has always been in flux. In the ancient world sex workers were usually sanctioned by the state and protected by law, and though they may not have been respected they were accepted. However, patriarchal and puritanical stances developed in the West by the sixteenth century. For example, in Augsburg after 1508 cockatrices, the euphemism attached to prostitutes, had their noses cut off if they were found soliciting on Holy Days. The criminalisation of prostitution in parts of Europe during this century forced the trade underground thereby creating dangerous working conditions. This happened in Southwark in 1545 towards the end of this part of the Tudor period.[5]

It is difficult to research the details of sexual practices within brothels during this period as there is no unbiased testimony of everyday people. We know the opinions of doctors and moralists, but, to my knowledge, we do not have sources representing the voices of sex workers themselves from the early sixteenth century. However, we know the stews existed and how they were organised and we can look at laws related to sex such as the 1533 Buggery Act and how it came to be issued.

To cast back in time, during the thirteenth century there were thirty-two bathhouses in Paris and eighteen in London. Smaller towns also had them. Sex was at the heart of a good deal of public bathing. In fact, sex and bathing were so closely related that phrases such as 'lather up' became sixteenth-century expressions for ejaculation. The medieval word for a brothel was a stew which derives from bathhouses.[6] William Langham's *Garden of Health* of 1579 recommends adding rosemary to a bath: 'Seethe much rosemary and bathe therein to make thee lusty, lively, joyful, liking and youngly.'[7] Musk harvested from the glands of a civet cat became a luxury item in the stews, along with castor from the anal glands of a beaver and ambergris (which is whale vomit). Lavender, as mentioned in an earlier chapter, was frequently associated with illicit Tudor sex, and harlots often smelled of it.

Women in bathhouses used homemade, and often dangerous dilapidory creams, and whores plucked their eyebrows. An abundance of pubic hair on the other hand was a sign of youth, health and sexual vitality. However, pubic lice could only be eliminated by shaving and this is where the merkin emerges. This was a pubic hair wig which first appeared in 1450, according to the Oxford Companion to the Body.[8] A well-thatched prostitute might be more desirable than a shaved one. Equally, a merkin might be looked upon as signifying disease, concealing the effects of mercury used to treat syphilis. It could, of course, be titillating if tied in place with a silky fine ribbon.

The earliest evidence of venereal protection resembling a condom appeared during the Tudor era. A sheep's intestine turned into a condom was used on occasion, mainly to prevent catching syphilis during coitus with a prostitute. Fish bladders were also used. The gut would be cut to size and dried out, requiring soaking in milk or water in order to rehydrate. They, like merkins, would be fastened to the penis with a ribbon or string, washed out and reused later. It actually was not until the eighteenth century that condoms became a business enterprise.[9]

The stews of Southwark were where you might find the most notorious brothels of Tudor London. They were situated between Maiden Lane and Bankside, close to arenas for bull and bear baiting. They gained their name from the 'stew ponds' where the Bishop of Winchester bred his fish (*estuwes* also was the name of the stove used to heat water for the bathhouses). Southwark was outside the jurisdiction of the Lord Mayor of London and under rent control of the Bishopric of Winchester. During the Reformation the Catholic bishop's lands passed to the new Anglican Bishop of Winchester. Ironically, the Catholic bishop Stephen Gardiner cemented his relationship with the King by providing him with Winchester geese. This was the name given to Southwark prostitutes, which derives from the bishop's association with prostitutes (see later in this chapter).

The stews were closed for a while by King Henry VII in 1506 to halt the rising levels of syphilis. The thousands of prostitutes who were evicted from the brothels had no choice but to ply their trade in the streets.[10] A year later, though, they were reopened. On 13 April 1546 his son Henry VIII shut down the Southwark stews again, issuing a royal proclamation forcing the closure of all houses of prostitution in England. This did not end prostitution. In fact, it increased the practice within the City when the ladies moved over the river from Southwark into ale houses or other premises used for purposes other than selling sex.[11]

The stews were described in John Stow's *London* as whitewashed premises facing the Thames. He describes how the stew houses had signs on their fronts facing the river, not hung up but rather painted on the walls. One these, The Cardinal's Hat, was situated west of the Bear Garden and east of Great Pike Garden close, at number 49 Bankside. By 1542 it had been renamed The King's Head. The brothel had a continuous existence since 1360 and a poem of 1522 contains a reference to prostitution here. The poet John Skelton wrote the following verse in *Why Not Come to Court*:

> What news, what news
> But naked stews
> I understand how that
> The sign of The Cardinal's Hat
> That Inn is now shut up
> With gup/now gup.

He refers to a closure in 1522, suggesting that it had a temporary hiatus as a brothel prior to Henry VIII's proclamation of 1546 to cease state licensing.[12]

Single women working in the stews were forbidden the rites of the Church so long as they continued their sinful life. They were excluded from Christian burial if they were not reconciled before their death. A plot of ground called the Single Woman's Churchyard was appointed for them. Stow also describes the Bishop of Winchester's house in Southwark as 'a fair house, well repaired, and hath a large wharf and landing place called The Bishop's Stairs.' Interested merchants and nobleman must have landed there, ferried over the Thames, to visit the stews.[13]

\* \* \*

Many women were not able to marry because of a lack of a dowry and therefore had to support themselves. There may also have been too few men in a position to marry and thus offer them financial support. This would have resulted from men returning seriously wounded from wars, or not returning at all. The brothel, therefore, was a means to financial survival for women and regulations from 1350 until 1550 echoed society's tolerance of brothels here and elsewhere in Europe. Municipal authorities recognised the social value of prostitution, placing it under strict control rather than banning it, which led to the growth of of licensed red-light districts in European towns and cities. Stews also fulfilled a demand and were a source of income for many towns. Furthermore, they were also believed to prevent male homosexuality, rape and seduction.

In Europe regulations meant prostitutes would wear distinguishing clothing or were forbidden to wear certain types of clothing or jewellery. They could not attend church nor could they speak to respectable women. Some towns had restrictions on who could visit a brothel. In theory no clerics, married men or Jews could enter therein but of course this was not enforced.[14]

Officially regulated brothels were not the rule everywhere in England, though Southwark's brothels did have much in common with regulations in Europe. Boroughs in England had their own courts and systems with fines in place for offences. Secular courts dealt with sexual offences that affected public order such as prostitution, rape, adultery and fornication. The only surviving records concerning actual prostitution are the texts of municipal regulations and court records. Courts could connect the presence of sex workers to taverns or gaming houses. Both these places were unacceptable and officially forbidden haunts for prostitutes so pimps or procurers placed individual working women in taverns rather than groups of prostitutes. Many such procurers actually worked in a higher level of the trade than that of the typical brothel keeper. For instance they might operate for an individual customer rather than running an open house or brothel.

The authorities tried to keep prostitution in the stews of Southwark with the exception of London's Cock Lane. Before the closure, stew managers had to persuade the authorities they kept an honest stew. Interestingly, if prostitutes congregated in brothels they did not necessarily live under the supervision of a brothel keeper but rather in their own lodgings. Legislation from the era surviving for the Southwark stews presents the best picture of how stews could operate.[15] For example, the law did not allow brothel keepers a free hand over their sex workers.

All stew holders were supposed to be men accompanied by their wives. No unmarried woman could keep a stew house and men often owned the brothels women ran. Fines administered from 1505–06, however, show that women did own stew houses, and a 1519 list of suspicious persons arrested there notes the keeper of each house, several of whom were women. Accusations against women in 1519 range from thirty-four to fifty-nine per cent of total accusations. Brothel keeping was an important area of female entrepreneurship. If a couple owned a brothel only the man could be accused of running the brothel, assuming legalities referring to brothel-keeping were evaded. Equally, a man might be fined for activities carried out by his wife alone, those legal evasions with which he was not involved.

Prostitutes generally had to have their actual abode elsewhere and could not live in the stews. The brothel keeper merely rented premises to them for work. In the Southwark brothels, for instance, each woman had to pay fourteen pence a week for the use of her room. Stew holders could also rent rooms by the night to couples even if the woman did not work there, and there are references of men taking women to the stews.

Southwark regulations prevented a stew holder from overcharging the sex workers but in practice these regulations were breached. A prostitute could leave the stews any time she wished, even if a legal action against her was pending, but the bishop's officials were still required to regularly search for women being kept against their will. A few notorious cases are worth noting. In 1490 Henry Whitehere was accused in ecclesiastical courts of soliciting women to fornicate with other men. He took a woman named Margaret to the stews side of the river and sold her to a procurer. In 1517 John Barton was accused of taking a young girl, who was on her first visit to London, to the stews. There he made contact with a 'bawd' to sell her.[16] The victim managed to escape, aided by the wife of a waterman with whom Barton left her while he went off to negotiate price with a brothel keeper. Barton was convicted and sentenced to the pillory.

Other rules for regulating the stews include the following: a stew holder officially could not sell food or other goods in his house, nor could he keep a boat to ferry clients over the river to his brothel; any woman with the 'burning sickness' (syphilis) was banished. The City of London, as on the Continent, had regulations about certain types of clothing such as striped hoods which prostitutes had to wear. However, the Southwark brothels had no such restrictions on clothing. In 1538 the City complained about 'the evil example of the gorgeous apparel of common women' from the stews. This set an example of temptation to young women, wives and apprentices. A prostitute was not permitted to keep a paramour, nor could she support such a person financially. Punishments included prison, a fine, the cucking stool and banishment.

The church condemned prostitution and brothel keeping but this did not deter the Bishop of Winchester from sanctioning and regulating brothels in Southwark. Fines from the stews contributed to the bishop's income and this led to the encouragement of brothels as both prostitutes and stew holders paid fines for violations of regulations. The bishop had exclusive jurisdiction and this made Southwark brothels legal. In reality, though, brothel keepers were able to ignore the law as they were often under the protection of powerful citizens who owned the property and a landlord who charged a high rent could profit very well.

\* \* \*

In 1546 when all bathhouses and brothels were closed down[17] many prostitutes moved into private houses that sold alcohol as a cover and abuse was not unknown. In 1550 a London haberdasher, Middleton, was taken to court for letting his wife , their daughter and a ten-year-old serving maid have sex with Nicholas Hard, a gentleman. By the Elizabethan era brothels were explicitly associated with ale houses and known as 'slaughter houses', 'shambles', and 'block houses of the Devil'.

Another unappealing option for prostitutes following the closure of bathhouses and brothels was the workhouse. Mary I had ordered treadmills to be brought into the workhouses so that prostitutes could grind corn. They were also employed to beat out hemp with heavy wooden mallets. One such workhouse was Bridewell, which was granted a charter in 1553 as a workhouse for poor and idle persons of the City. Bridewell was labelled 'a godly foundation' and any women working there became labelled 'Bridewell baggage.'[19] A rhyme of the time runs as follows:

> The stews of England bore a beastly sway
> till the eighth Henry banished them away.
> And since these common whores were quite put down,
> a damned crue of private whores are grown
> so that the Devil will be doing still,
> either with public or private will.

By the mid sixteenth century rural depopulation, urban decay, price rises and falling wages led to an increase in poverty. Prostitution, which had begun in bathhouses during the Middle Ages, and was later regulated in brothels, thrived in places throughout the City of London and in Petticoat Lane, Smithfield, Shoreditch, Westminster, Clerkenwell, Whitefriars, Liberties, St Martin le Grand, and in Ave Maria Alley near St Pauls.[20] Women worked in waterfront taverns, loitered in churches, and worked alone for repeat clients who might pay for them to be lodged in houses that let out rooms to prostitutes. These became known as naughty houses and landlords made a good living renting out rooms.

\*    \*    \*

Illicit sex is defined in this book as any sexual relationship outside the traditional husband and wife marriage, such as homosexuality, adultery, clerical sex, concubines, pre-marital sex, sodomy, rape and incest. Prostitution was perceived as a necessary evil by Saint Thomas Aquinas who wrote: 'physical pleasures because of their intensity needed to be controlled and checked.'[21] Prostitution, as we have seen, was regulated.

All sorts of sexual activity forbidden by Canon law or deemed morally wrong by ecclesiastical authorities in Catholic Europe were also disapproved of by Tudor Church reformers. Women and prostitutes, too, were punished for illicit sex. Terms such as whore, meretrix and prostitute were used by society to shame scandalous women. Women who worked in taverns were called bawds and procuresses whether or not they had connection with the sex industry. An 'incontinent woman' was one who lacked self-control over sexual desire. In Oxford the chancellor's court recommended such women be banished from towns to protect the moral integrity of residents.

Different towns dealt differently with prostitution. In London, women were put in a pillory or had a hot rod placed in their hands before finally having their hair cut off and being expelled. Sometimes women were forced to wear striped hoods, an attempt by ecclesiastical courts to control social order and prevent sinful women from corrupting respectable citizens.[22] There was little consistency in England and on the Continent for punishing repeat offenders. The punishments for the most part involved fines, banishment and penance. On the Continent, Houses of Refuge took women in who were subsequently known as White Ladies.

Humiliation was also used as punishment for illicit sex. In 1562 in St Simon and Jude's Parish, Fye Bridge Street, Cambridge, the eighteen-year-old Benet Gedwyis was accused of whoredom and forced to ride on a cart, 'with a paper on her head and tinkled with a bason and so at one o'clock to be had at the cokyng stool and ducked in the water.' At this point a local onlooker removed the paper from Benet's head and threw it in the river, watched by the alderman's wife and by the public. This makes one wonder if the public considered her punishment overly harsh.[23] After the Reformation punishments became very public. Women could face the cucking stool like poor Benet.

Visitations to monasteries during the 1530s attempted, among other misconducts, to root out illicit sexual behaviour. Clerical sex, concubinage and involvement with prostitutes was one of the targets. Thomas Wolsey was long dead by then but he had several children by a mistress. After the reformation clergy were permitted to marry, as they had done in the Anglo-Saxon era. This law was briefly reversed by Mary I. Here, once again, we can observe Tudor dual standards but the thinking was that it was better they were wed than cohabiting with sex workers or taking mistresses.

Many of the clergy were believed to be the clients of prostitutes. After all, Grope Lanes, where illicit prostitution would occur were often situated near religious houses.[24] There was a crackdown on prostitution in the offing by the late 1530s, particularly in college towns. From 1535–1540 Thomas Cromwell, who orchestrated the closure of the monasteries, was Chancellor of Cambridge University and sent out inquisitors, though he was not the first to do so. This had happened periodically throughout previous centuries. As early as 1317 Edward II, after a request from the then Chancellor of Cambridge University, called upon local authorities to clamp down on prostitution and banish prostitutes from university towns. During the 1530s students were fined and could be ejected from their college if caught visiting brothels. Thomas Cromwell toiled hard to control fornication and adultery amongst students, clergy and the townspeople of Cambridge.[25]

The Grace Books are Church documents which record the inquisition associated with prostitution at the Stourbridge Fair in Cambridge.

Proctors from the university colleges inquired and listed searches for vagabonds, night-wanderers and others, including prostitutes. Individual punishments were not listed but in 1533 they were all expelled from the neighbourhood. During the 1530s the ecclesiastical courts still had jurisdiction in cases of fornication and adultery.[26]

Cases of bigamy were also reported in court records. On 4 July 1490 Thomas Hoke and Elizabeth requested a dispensation to permit their marriage even though they had married without being unmarried. The couple, who lived in Hereford, had married and had children even though her first husband, another Thomas, was still alive. When her first husband died they requested absolution from adultery and a dispensation for their marriage. They had lived together openly before the dispensation was requested. Couples like them tended to live openly together and wait until the first partner died to legitimise relationships. Dispensations were also sought when a child resulted from a priest having an affair or even a secret wife.[27]

\* \* \*

It is more difficult to explore male prostitution. Without doubt it did exist. Under Henry VIII's rule The Buggery Act would have sent this deep underground. However, to illustrate its existence there is the documented case of a male transvestite prostitute working between London and Oxford during the last decade of the fourteenth century. This suggests that clergy and students engaged in such illicit sex. The man, Rykener, was arrested in London for wearing women's clothing and engaging in sex with another man in 1394. He admitted to relations with two Franciscans at The Swan Inn, Burford. In the same month and same place he had sex with another friar and six travellers. He claimed to have had sex with many nuns as a man and sex with many women too, married or otherwise.[28]

There has always been sex, and as Kate Lister points out in *A Curious History of Sex*, if not actually the world's oldest profession, since midwifery wins heads down, sex is 'the oldest currency.' We have always traded sex and, as it was so in Tudor times, attitudes to the sex trade are constantly fluid. Women's sexuality did come in for particular censure, particularly during the Reformation. Women's sexuality was disparaged but women who peddled sex for coin were censured by society.

*Aphrodisiacs and Love Potions*

An aphrodisiac is a food, drink or drug that increases libido and enhances sexual pleasure and performance. These aids to sexual performance have been recorded throughout history. One of the earliest treatments for impotence appears in an ancient Hindu text known as *Sushruta Samhita* c.600 BC. It suggests powders of sesame and sali rice should be mixed with saindhara salt and a quantity of the juice of sugar cane mixed with hog's lard and cooked with clarified butter.[1]

Medieval and Tudor people believed the food they consumed could influence their sex lives; it was all part of the humoral notion. They thought, according to medical theory, that food and drink was one of the things on which health should depend. A poor diet could cause illness but a patient could be restored to health by changes in diet, which sounds rather familiar. However, they also believed that food and drink could solve sexual problems including impotence and infertility. Medieval medical texts contained references to foods and sexual advice for the late medieval man.[2]

Constantine the African was a translator of Arabic medieval texts into Latin. He lived in Salerno, Italy's medical centre during the medieval era. His text on human fertility, *De Coitu*, has a section on foods and herbs which provoke desire. These were foods that were likely to generate semen and incite a man to intercourse. He also suggested foods to dry up and diminish semen so that men could eat according to whichever condition they suffered, too much desire or too little of it.

Medieval doctors, and this applies during the sixteenth century also, believed semen was a processed form of blood and therefore derived from food. Three types of food were conducive to the production of semen and were grouped as nourishing foods, foods especially windy and foods that are warm and moist. Chickpeas contain all three and were considered an aphrodisiac. Other foods they thought drew out and produced semen were fresh meat, pepper, wine, brains, and egg yolks. However, cold foods such as fish, cucumber and lettuce might repress, impede or thicken semen and therefore destroy lust.[3]

Aphrodisiac recipes were included in handbooks and regimes to help Tudor men with their sexual problems. Cloves in milk and blueberry juice, the brains of small sparrows, grease surrounding the kidneys of a freshly killed billy goat, all these might treat impotence. On the other hand, rue, powdered and added to a potion, could be drunk to dry out sperm, and the juice of water lilies taken for forty days might take care of the over-sexed problem. An anophrodisiac, the opposite of an aphrodisiac, was intended to supress libido and impair sexual function. Anophrodisiacs fell into three categories: starving the body, cooling the body and sedating the body. Sedating might be achieved through fasting and rigorous exercise. Early Christian saints regularly fasted to purify the body and monks would starve for long periods to control their sexual hunger and desire for food.

*Regimen Studies* by Maino de Maineri suggests the man who wished to avoid the production of semen and repress lust should make use of cold foods such as lentil water cooled with cauliflower seeds, water lily and lettuce seeds, lettuce water made slightly vinegary, or seeds of purslane.[4] Camphor was considered useful to dry out lustful parts and if rubbed on the penis might keep the member flaccid.

Spicy hot food could inflame the senses but cucumbers were cool and bland and even though phallic in shape were considered an effective anophrodisiac. In the sixteenth century Francis Rabelais suggested, in addition to the benefits of water lily seeds, willow twigs, hemp stalks, woodbine, honeysuckle, tamarisk, mandrake, and the dried out skin of a hippo. In a way, Rabelais was sending up medieval quackery.[5]

The oyster is the most well-known and enduring of aphrodisiacs. During the sixteenth century oysters came into their own as a libido-enhancing culinary food. In 1566 Alain Chartier suggested oysters 'doe provoke lecherie.'[6] Pickled oysters were sold in brothels in 1646. It is likely they were also sold in brothels during the previous century as a sex-inducing food. This no doubt stems from the fact that an oyster has a resemblance to the vulva with soft folds of pink, salty flesh with nestling pearls. It was slang for vulva during the sixteenth century and later the figure of an oyster girl selling them on the streets became associated with sex workers.

There has been no scientific evidence that oysters are an aphrodisiac although they are a healthy food. Shellfish, though, are associated with Aphrodite-Venus who was allegedly born from the sea and appears in Botticelli's *Birth of Venus*. According to the Greek poet Hesiod, Aphrodite rose from waves fully formed after Uranus's testicles were thrown into the sea by Cronus. The myth is possibly the provenance for how shellfish acquired a sexy reputation. Sparrows were also associated with Aphrodite and they, too, became regarded as a potent aphrodisiac in the Classical world. Recipes in the *Karma Sutra* to excite passion also feature sparrow eggs.[7]

Apricots were a new Renaissance food introduced into England. They were alleged to contain aphrodisiac traits. This may have been because of a signature visual link between them and the genitals. Think, too, of the word's syllables – a/pric/ot. The apricot would have to be pulled from the stem to be eaten. Another food associated with sex is the asparagus which, as noted in Classical writings and much loved by Tudor humanists, could incite the body towards desire.[8]

Sugar was a favourite item, believed to have medicinal qualities (candied roses were thought to cure gonorrhoea) and to be an aphrodisiac.[9] It was so valuable it was kept in a block under lock and key and was the preserve of elite households. Sugar was made into gorgeously decorated plates and goblets, the plates containing marzipan sweets. It is amazing to think of items made entirely of sugar and what it did to Tudor teeth.

Love potions have always been around though following the Reformation they went underground as people might be accused of witchcraft for administering them. Spanish fly, for example, is an emerald green chemical derived from blister beetles and was administered, crushed, in tonics. It could apparently cause feelings of warmth and intense sexual desire to course through the body. This ingredient, however, was dangerous and rumoured to have caused the death of Catherine of Aragon's father, Ferdinand of Aragon. Ferdinand remarried after the death of his wife, Isabella of Castile. It was thought that due to his advancing years, and having married the much younger Germain of Foix, he wanted to increase his virility and therefore ingested many suspicious elixirs containing Spanish fly. Flowers, too, were used as love potions. One love charm was to plant marigolds in the footsteps where the object of one's love had walked. Mashed worms and herbs could work equally as well. Sacramental bread, believed to turn into the body of Christ during the rite of the Eucharist, was also considered to possess magical qualities to aid love.

Saint Luke was the revered patron saint of artists, physicians and bachelors and was often called upon to help people find their soulmates. On 18 October, the saint's feast day, a mixture of herbs, vinegar and honey might be anointed upon the head before going to bed. The prayer of St Luke would be said because, hopefully, one's beloved would appear in a dream: 'St Luke, St Luke, be kind to me, in my dreams let me my true love see.'[10]

Sweaty cakes, made from blood and bodily fluids, might be presented to an intended lover. The cakes were believed to make one fall head over heels in love. Bits of skin and hair from an intended couple could be mixed into a brew to promote amorous feelings.[11] And not forgetting that long-forgotten Tudor vegetable, which is now grown at Hampton Court. The skirrat is similar to a parsnip or carrot. It has fluffy, white, parsley-like leaves with white flowers. John Warlidge, gentleman and gardener, wrote in 1677, 'By physicians, it is deemed a great restorative and good for weak stomachs and an effectual friend to Dame Venus.'[12]

# Chapter 9

# Sex and Witchcraft

One of the accusations levied against Anne Boleyn by Elizabethan Catholic writers and seventeenth-century writers concerning her trial in May 1536 was that of witchcraft. Anne, it was said, had bewitched King Henry. She was unconventionally dark-haired and dark-eyed when it was more popular in this era to be fair of colouring and blond. Seventeenth-century historians alleged that she had an extra finger which she concealed carefully beneath long sleeves, suggesting this to be a witch's mark. Had she bewitched King Henry into marrying her and, moreover, the young men accused in 1536 of falling in love with her?[1] There is plenty of historical fiction using precisely this notion within their narratives, but Anne Boleyn was not accused of witchcraft at her trial.

People did fear witchcraft during the Tudor era and beyond, but this fear did not reach its hysterical peak in England until the seventeenth century, so it is not surprising that this accusation was levelled at Anne Boleyn by later historians. During the days of Henry VIII England swarmed with astrologers and sorceresses. High and low persons alike consulted them without fear. Even Henry himself lent an ear to foolish prophesies and old wives' chantings. He did give out the opinion that he had made his marriage to Anne seduced by witchcraft, but this was not, as pointed out above, an accusation made by him at his queen's trial.

Waves of persecutions of homosexuals in sixteenth-century Europe seem to correlate with the persecution of accused witches. Both homosexuals and witches were considered dangerous deviants whose existence threatened the wellbeing of society. Women were traditionally regarded as temptresses, taking after their ancestral Eve. They were thought to have followed Eve's fickleness and, therefore, were a liability towards sexual arousal. This was, of course, to the late sixteenth-century Tudor, a threat to family life,[2] and witchcraft was often associated with unacceptable sexual activity.

Neighbours were ever watchful. Life in villages was traditionally controlled by community decisions in the manorial court. Domestic life in a village was overshadowed by the growth of neighbourly activity and scrutiny and everyone gossiped freely. The only safe way to manoeuvre oneself through this closed world was by exceptional self-control, outward reserve, secrecy and duplicity. The English village during the early Tudor era could be a belligerent and hot-blooded place. Neighbours peeked through windows and there were plenty of busybodies ready to report on any activity they considered deviant or inappropriate.[3] Every village had its wise woman who lived alone, often with a cat for company, and who were often among the first to be accused.

*Malleus Maleficarum* means the practice of harmful magic or witchcraft. The associated book called *The Hammer of the Witches* was published in 1486. It was written by the Catholic clergyman Heinrich Kramer using his Latin name, Henricus Institoris. This book elevated sorcery to the criminal status of heresy and recommended witches be tortured in order to get confessions and if (when) convicted be subject to the death penalty;[4] i.e., burning at the stake.

Before 1400 it was rare for anyone to be persecuted for witchcraft but by the fifteenth century belief in witches was widespread. Persecution was brutal after the publication of the book, which, due to the invention of the printing press, was then circulated widely. Scribed in Latin, there were fourteen editions released between 1487 and 1520 and sixteen further editions released between 1574 and 1669. They were issued from leading printing presses in Germany, France and Italy.

Within the pages of *The Hammer of the Witches* was a series of questions and answers, or suggestions as to how to identify and deal with witches. For example, relevant to sex and sexuality, Question 3, Part 1 poses the question: 'Whether children can be generated by incubi and succubi, devils and other malignant magical creatures.' In response to its own question, the text argues that devils interfere in the process of normal copulation and conception by obtaining human semen and themselves transferring it. They can assume a human body to pass on semen to another person. It further suggests that devils have a power stronger than humans and can change people's will, forcing them perform witchcraft undiscovered.

Lecherous satyrs and fauns called incubi were believed to appear to wanton women and persuade them to copulate with them. The wildman of the woods, or woodwose, was another mythical figure well known to Tudor villagers. He was like a faun or satyr and was akin to Silvanus, the Roman god of woodlands. He was depicted in art as covered with hair and can be seen on intersecting carved and painted roof bosses in Canterbury Cathedral. The woodwose can also be found in many churches in Suffolk where mysterious carvings of them can be found on the staves of stone baptismal fonts or reliefs decorating the porch of a church. Folk traditions associated with him were connected to the desire to capture him and release him in exchange for his wisdom. By the Tudor era the wildman of the woods was connected with mining and during the sixteenth century may have inspired the fairy tale *Beauty and the Beast*.

Another question in the Malleus asks 'Why is it Women are chiefly addicted to evil superstitions?' The book speaks of the sort of women most susceptible to witchcraft, including midwives. The female sex was perceived as fragile and as a consequence more witches would be female than male. *The Hammer of Witches* suggests that if women are governed by a good spirit they are excellently virtuous but if women were governed by a bad spirit they would be full of vice. The book quotes Ecclesiasticus XXV : 'No head above the head of a serpent and no wrath above the wrath of a woman.' Women were considered more carnal in nature than men.

A Papal Bull of 1481 gave official endorsement to the misguided zeal expressed in *The Hammer of Witches*. A judge in Lorraine, for example, one Nicholas Remy, claimed to have burned 900 witches during the 1580s. British attitudes to witchcraft were less extreme during the fifteenth and sixteenth centuries than those of their European neighbours. Sometimes an English witch was considered acceptable and perhaps even an almost respectable member of society, but acceptance was not universal. Those wise women or midwives who attracted adverse attention during Mary I's reign could end up tried for their 'crimes'.[5] These could be a potion gone wrong or a stillbirth, or even, on occasion, the birth of twins. Some believed twins must be conceived with two different fathers suggesting their mother was a loose unfaithful woman.

English witchcraft tests tended to favour the accuser. Ducking the accused witch in the village pond was one such test in which the guilty floated and the innocent sank or were pulled to safety by ropes. The accused could be weighed against the Bible. If the Bible was heavier the accused was a witch.

The usual death for an English witch was by hanging, not burning. The crimes that were the most common reasons for a witch trial included souring milk, inflicting death or disease, causing miscarriage, cursing or hurting children. Tudor England was full of 'cunning women'. They were white magicians, typically harmless, who sold charms to help people overcome problems, including in matters of love. Typical of these were charms or ornaments to ward off evil, stave off ruin or make money. Rings were sold to bring immunity in battle, keep off vermin and even make the wearer invisible. White magicians were tolerated during the early Tudor era because they provided healing advice, or might discover lost possessions, and they could also mix sought-after love potions. Country people could not afford doctors and often looked to the wise woman for medical help.

The European witch, meanwhile, might confess under torture to having intercourse with the devil and suckling demons at her breast. The accused would be stripped and searched for tell-tale marks and tortured to extract a full confession. The discovery of a birthmark or extra nipple became a key factor in determining a witch's guilt.

\* \* \*

In England by 1542 witchcraft was defined as a felony by Henry VIII's Witchcraft Act, a crime that was punishable by death as well as forfeiture of all goods and chattels. It was forbidden to:

> use devise practise or exercise, or cause to be devised practised or exercised, any invocations or conjurations of sprites, witchcrafts or sorceries to the intent to find money or treasure or to waste consume or destroy any person in his body members, or to provoke any person to unlawful love, or for any other unlawful intent or purpose [...] or for dig up or pull down any cross or crosses by such invocations or conjurings of sprites witchcrafts, enchantments or sorceries or any of them take upon them to tell or declare where goods stolen or lost shall become.[6]

This statute was repealed by Henry's son, Edward VI, in 1547, but it was not repealed for long. During the Elizabethan era the Act of 1562 against Conjurations, Enchantments and Witchcrafts demanded the death penalty where harm had been caused. If anyone was killed or harmed as a result of witchcraft the death penalty came into play. Lesser offences led to imprisonment.

The British, or English, witch usually kept a familiar such as a dog, cat or toad. One interesting witch trial involved Elizabeth Francis, wife of Hatfield Peverell, who was charged at the Chelmsford summer assizes of 1566 with bewitching the infant child of William Auger. She had learned the art of witchcraft from her grandmother, one named as Mother Eve, at the age of twelve. Elizabeth had been given a cat named Satan to help her seduce Andrew Byles but when he refused to marry her she was accused of having caused his death. Her accusers believed that her cat quickly found her a husband with whom she had a daughter. When the child was eighteen months old, Elizabeth, as accused, had ordered her cat to kill the girl. Elizabeth, probably terrified, denied this but confessed to ordering Satan to make her husband, Christopher, lame. After she had owned Satan for fifteen years, it was mooted that Elizabeth grew tired of her cat and gave him to a neighbour, Agnes Waterhouse. Agnes was, as a consequence, also charged with practicing witchcraft in 1566. When Elizabeth claimed she was innocent of the specific charge against her, she was sentenced to a year in jail. She received another year for bewitching a neighbour called Mary Cocke, and later she made four appearances in the pillory. By 1579 Elizabeth was on trial yet again and this time was found guilty of bewitching Anne Poole who died the year before. This time, Elizabeth was hanged.

In July 1589 three witches were hanged at Chelmsford Essex. One was a woman called Joan Prentice who was later depicted on pamphlets as having suckled familiars, including two rat-like ferrets called Jack and Jill.

\*    \*    \*

It was not until after James I came to the throne in 1603 with his utter fear of the supernatural that the witch-hunting obsession in England really got underway.[7]

Before the Reformation people believed that saints could protect against witchcraft. Saint Sebastian, for instance, was favoured because of his wounds. He protected against the plague. St Barbara protected against storms which were associated with witchcraft, and, of course, the Virgin Mary protected everyone. Throughout the era there was a blurred line between magic and legitimate medical practice in people's minds. Poor and unprotected women, but particularly the cunning women, were the main victims of Tudor witch hunts. By the end of the Tudor period the execution of a witch was a ritual that enjoyed the approval of an entire village community. Many Tudors thought that if there were no witches there would be no plagues, that curses would not cause harm and death could not be caused to an unwilling suitor by an enchantress. Without doubt, however, love potions continued to be peddled by many surviving village wise women. Healing potions were sold to impoverished citizens, and after the English Reformation more frequently to those deprived of the medical help that had once offered by the recently dissolved monasteries.

## Chapter 10

# Renaissance Art and Sex

D uring the Renaissance the rise of Humanism and an increased sense of human individuality encouraged artists to glance back at Classical art and literature with a new vision. For instance, in a book written in 1532 by Greg Proctor, *Mythological Theology*, it was revealed that a Venus statue with a beard and penis existed in ancient times on Cyprus and that cross-dressing men and women would sacrifice to the bi-gendered deity.[1] Venus appears frequently in Renaissance painting and as female. *The Birth of Venus* by Sandro Botticelli, 1445–1510, is an obvious example.

A notion existed during the Renaissance that viewing a beautiful painting could elevate the viewer higher up the spiritual plane. Painting became naturalistic and more realistic during this time and painters would use their skills to create images that appeared in three dimensions. Leonardo da Vinci, for example, used this new concept to define the relationship of apparently three-dimensional figures.[2]

Non-religious paintings flourished during the Renaissance in addition to religious painting. Their artists followed humanist thinking, using Greek and Roman mythology as inspiration. There was, however, a conservative backlash. In 1493 an Italian priest Savanola was so outraged by what he saw as corruption he commanded the destruction of many such paintings during the Florence Carnival, an event that became known as 'The Bonfire of the Vanities'. Merchants' daughters caused offence to the conservatives as they often entered marriages with traditional trousseau chests painted with pagan stories and images from myths such as Paris and Helen of Troy and Venus/Aphrodite.

\*   \*   \*

By the sixteenth century Christendom was connected to a great wider world. From the thirteen century onwards the Christian Crusader states in the Holy Land were recaptured by the Muslim kingdoms and Eastern ideas moved west when the Franks returned to Europe. Columbus reached the New World in 1492. This impacted on art. Artists travelled within and between countries more than previously. A network of European courts facilitated their movement and at the same time works of theological and philosophical thought connected with antiquity became a pan-European trend that was not limited to Italy, the birthplace of Renaissance thinking and art.

Before 1500 art did not simply suggest painting. Sculpture and tapestry were viewed as art and more likely to be placed on display in a gallery within great palaces. Art that had been previously held mostly in the hands of the Church now had wealthy secular owners. A ruler, institution or an individual such as the Duke of Milan, as well as Henry VII and Henry VIII became avid collectors of tapestries as well as paintings, often displaying sexy pastoral scenes woven in silken, linen and wool threads.

The wealthy began to spend money on both artefacts and dynastic portraits and so it became a part of social elitism to be a collector or a patron of the arts. Thomas Cromwell, the English king's first minister, enjoyed all things Italian, having spent his youthful years in Florence and Venice where he rubbed shoulders with Renaissance artists and sculptors. An inventory of his home at Austin Friars indicates he had a substantial collection of Renaissance inspired objects. For example, his parlour and hall were graced with the representations of Lucretia Romana. The good and righteous Lucretia was desired by the sexually insatiable Prince Tarquin, whose conduct brought about the fall of the Roman monarchy. Inside one of his parlours was a cloth showing images of lovers, a man and a woman.[3]

Hans Holbein was employed as a court painter in England. Tudors enjoyed small portraits, miniatures known as limnings, as well as having their larger portraits. It is from this era on that we can actually see what our kings and queens looked like. Before the Tudor era religious art was in existence to convey both doctrine and religious stories. This was, in particular, aimed towards the ordinary medieval person who could not read. Carvings of kings and queens we see on Cathedral bosses were not intended to represent a medieval king or queen with accuracy. Various religious art was there for adornment, with animals such as serpents and birds providing simple enjoyment for the viewer. They could look at paintings on walls and pillars in churches with reflection, at least until many of these were eliminated by Protestant decree during the Reformation. Times were changing for the arts too during the sixteenth century. Painting acquired a new elite status meaning that court painters such as Holbein would travel extensively from court to court and country to country seeking portraiture commissions from wealthy patrons.[4]

How does Renaissance art connect to Tudor sex and sexuality? Art does so in many ways but a modern-day viewer should be aware that the world of the sixteenth century possessed a different mindset. Looking at these paintings with a possession of twenty-first century mores, one might perceive sexual messages which, while present, are not entirely the message we should expect to interpret. Renaissance art needs to be viewed as if we are time travelling in order to grasp their meaning better. What we might perceive as sexual can have another provenance.

Take Renaissance images of men. They present a sense of sensuality and masculinity, but instead of overt sexuality they actually show images of male bonding. These paintings present a civic, familial and patriarchal sense that is non-threatening. Sixteenth-century portraits offer idealised notions of masculinity that were, at the time of painting, over-determined. They emphasise virility, which is not surprising in an era that was misogynistic. Questions might arise for the twenty-first century viewer: could a young man be aroused by images of active masculine figures like Henry VIII's much-loved Hercules, or portraits of muscular soldiers, or Donatello's bronze David? Could Renaissance men be titillated by any number of portraits offering narcissistic pleasure?[5] Paintings of women were filtered through ideas of beauty and propriety often disguised as pious imitations of female saints, the Madonna herself or as sexy nymphs and goddesses such as Flora. Again, the Renaissance love of such painting and sculpture was tied up with public display and social roles.

Role-playing portraiture became very popular at this time, suggesting fantasy to viewers rather than overt sexuality. For instance, Cosimo I de' Medici, was disguised as the lover, Orpheus, in one painting that he commissioned from Agnolo Bronzino (1503–1572). Cosimo had himself painted for his new bride, Eleanora of Toledo. There is an icy sensuality in this portrait of Cosimo. Orpheus was, after all, the magical charmer, devoted lover, philosopher and peacemaker; he was the mortal who, interestingly, discovered male to male love. However, this portrait bypasses stereotypes of either homosexuality or heterosexuality because the elongated fingers suggest arousal, a delivery of teasing play eroticising the naked ruler's body. His portrait as Orpheus is more about virility, strength and beauty than sex.[6]

Young men of the time liked to be portrayed as beautiful, with extravagant refinement. This was considered acceptable rather than shameful. Such art parades heterosexuality, tempting viewers with the sight of male adolescent flesh. Vernacular language from the period including pretty boy, sweet boy, beardless youth sees young males as passive objects of desire to be admired from a distance. These young rulers were all very vain but also extremely proud of their virility and ability to continue their dynasties.

Symbolism enters such paintings. A lizard, for instance, was a symbol of shyness or coolness in love and of constancy. In Lotto's painting of a young man leaning on a table in his study there is the sense of loss and stoicism. Scattered about the sitter are objects suggesting romantic symbolism such as a lute, a hunting horn, a dead bird, keys placed on a storage shelf, an inkstand, letters, a green lizard, gloves, a gold chain, all suggesting rejection and a sense of lost love. Petals in the same portrait indicate the perishable fragility of youth and beauty. The sitter has the attractiveness of charisma, status and honour reminiscent of Christ's perfect beauty.

Mythological figures abound in Renaissance portraiture such as the painting of a shepherd in the collection at Hampton Court. It began as a formal portrait and was worked up to present this sitter in the guise of one of Virgil's shepherds. Figures were constantly masked with classical garb. Pastoral and sensual fantasies worked by Renaissance painters made Arcadian dreams imaginable. *La Bella* by Titian appears as an elaborate pin up and mildly erotic.

Portraits were more about same-sex friendships and the appreciation of physical beauty. The Raphael painting *Artist and Friend* shows an intricate balance between reserve, subordination, superior distance, absorbed narcissism and detached exclusion, with a tension between idealism and individualism. It is a play between two men in a complicated relationship, an example of Renaissance art that portrays men as humorous, decorative, sinful, and also arousing, yet its purpose was to amuse. The painting is filled with social ambiguity rather than being obviously heterosexual or in any way homosexual.[7]

*    *    *

Botticelli's *Birth of Venus* was completed in 1486. Venus was a hot subject for a Renaissance painter. This beautiful painting shows the goddess arriving in Cyprus. It was the first life-sized painting of a naked woman in the West and was destined to be copied and marketed for centuries.[8] She is placed in a Classical context. One of Venus's companions wears a girdle of myrtle and erect bulrushes represent the story's eroticism. A soft red cloak as well as roses present a nod to a mass of castrated matter from which, according to legend, Venus emerged. This painting is acknowledging physical and metaphysical beauty. It represents art as inspired by classical allegery, and it displays physical perfection. A fabulous painting such as *The Birth of Venus* would hang in the Renaissance villas of wealthy middle-class merchants and nobles. Venus was a beautiful woman, a partner in relationships, dominant as well as satisfying a male lover's desires. She became a cultural icon, a symbol of beauty and love, which, importantly, are overcoming urges of lust.[9] Renaissance painting and portraiture was more about aspiring to perfection than being sexy, though, without doubt, it cannot help being sexy too.

During the Tudor era Venus became represented as a favoured object of desire. The English nobility admired all things Italian. Italian art was imitated in the form of tapestry, wall painting, reliefs and even trinket boxes. Thomas Cromwell was a collector, and King Henry too. Shakespeare published his first poem *Venus and Adonis* during the Elizabethan era. In the poem Venus is a female consumed by desire who hunts down unhappy Adonis. Venus, a loved image throughout the Tudor age, morphs into the perfect woman, plump, fair and waiting to have sex. She was an impossible ideal for most Renaissance women. As suggested in *Le Miroir de la Beaute* by Louis Guyon, Venus should ideally be blond, in possession of a long neck, shining eyes, firm breasts and shapely hips, a plump but not wrinkled stomach, firm arms and bounteous buttocks.

In 1555 *Secreti de Reverendo* was published and translated into most European languages as well as being reissued in many editions. This beauty book encouraged women to achieve physical perfection with hair removal creams, hair dyes, anti-wrinkle lotions and milk, sugar and butter concoctions aimed at making the body smooth like that of a goddess. Venus was the most viewed naked female in the world by the Tudor era.[10] She was a 'sex and violence goddess', originally designed to explain the tempestuous and desirous side of human behaviour. 'In a region that spans modern day Iraq, Syria, Jordan, Lebanon, Turkey and Egypt, from at least 3000 BC onwards men and women watched one, another, and generated in their minds a sex-and-violence deity to explain the tempestuous and desirous nature of human behaviour'. Bettany Hughes refers to bone evidence from the time that tells us 'it was a time of violence and turbulence' and one with 'unbridled passions'. She suggests it was a world in which demi-gods and spirits were present everywhere. These savagely lusty deities were responsible for this continuing state. (Hughes, Bettany, *Venus & Aphrodite*, p15). Not so by the sixteenth century. Venus had shifted herself into a Renaissance image of love, beauty and desire.

Symbolism abounded in sixteenth-century paintings. One amusing and fascinating symbolic feature was that of the weasel. Weasels covered the whole of the mustelid family. They included ermine, sables, martens, ferrets and mink. Of interest specifically to Renaissance art, a widely-held belief was that weasels conceived though their ears and gave birth through their mouths. This gave rise to a language of hidden sexual symbolism in art with weasels symbolising everything from fertility talismans to phallic symbols. A sixteenth-century portrait by Leonardo da Vinci, *The Lady and the Ermine*, shows a young bride wearing an ermine, which was thought to bring good luck and help her get pregnant. In the painting the bride's hand rests over her lower abdomen and she holds the white ermine close to her womb. White weasels were symbols of sexual purity. The story goes that the ermine would rather give themselves up to a hunter than risk soiling their pristine fur in the chase. Da Vinci's white ermine attests to the purity of his subject, the pregnant sixteen-year-old mistress of the Duke of Milan. The duke belonged to a knighthood called the Order of the Ermine and a muscular weasel would indicate his virility.[11] Since weasels suggested fertility, weasel paintings became an ideal wedding gift.

In a marriage painting by Lavinia Fortana, a young Bolognese noble woman wears a red wedding gown. She pats a little dog which is white, the symbol of marital fidelity. Over her right arm she holds a weasel pelt with a jewelled head. This pelt was known as flea fur since it might distract fleas from the wearer's pristine skin. However, its inclusion represents the possibility and the hope that the bride will be fertile. Brides touching their wombs in paintings hope that God will bless them with a child. The idea connects with Christ's miraculous conception which happened when God's angel whispered into the ear of the Virgin.[12]

In the two partnered portraits of Pier Maria Rossi di San Secundo and that of his wife, Camilla Conzago, who is with their three sons, Camilla strokes a weasel. Pier has a codpiece that is prominent, just like Henry VIII in Holbein's portraits. In the painting of Camilla's husband, Camilla is gazing at her husband with extreme pride. She is surrounded by their sons and one son is staring at his father's codpiece. The symbolism only really works if the portraits are hung side by side. The father's large codpiece attests to the ideals of masculinity which the child aspires towards in adulthood.[13] A white ermine also appears in a portrait of Elizabeth I who was often referred to as the Virgin Queen. In this later painting a white weasel attests to the Queen's purity and unmarried status. It becomes a political statement suggesting Elizabeth is married only to her kingdom.

One folk belief was for a woman to wear a weasel's testicles around her neck or tie them to her thigh. In this way, a weasel as a symbol of sexual rampancy having been emasculated, might provide a potent counter-spell. The weasel represented purity in people's minds. Readers, choose your weasel. Will it be a fertility weasel, phallic weasel, a purity weasel or a success weasel? Whichever, they all made an appearance on wedding gifts and in paintings during the Tudor period. Including a weasel in a painting on tapestry or on an object would also be a way to indicate your high social status, and as a dual purpose the furry creature might just draw fleas away from your skin too.

\* \* \*

When the Tudors saw political possibilities of the new Renaissance interest in art they made full use of these. One way was to create sumptuous settings at court, reminding people of the King's wealth and power. The Tudors were not yet secure on the throne and were constantly striving for recognition as a new dynasty ever since the Battle of Bosworth in 1485.

The throne had changed hands through force six times during a period of eighty-six years thus the Tudors were determined to convince their subjects of their permanence.

Buildings were one way they expressed prestige and new innovation. Henry VIII was the greatest royal builder England has ever had. His father, Henry VII, built Sheen and renamed it Richmond and the Tudors had been Earls of Richmond. Henry VII built Greenwich Palace, rebuilt Baynard's Castle in London, and Henry VIII built and improved even older palaces along Renaissance lines as well as building beautiful new palaces and hunting lodges such as Nonesuch in Surrey. Portraits became the fashion in England and they would hang on the walls of long galleries in these modern palaces. Art during the period began to add to the prestige of the King and the nation.

During the Middle Ages artists were perceived as mere craftsmen. Gothic art was mainly about putting over a usually religious message rather than presenting an image of the real world. Previously a king would be drawn larger than the other figures in a decorative picture in a medieval manuscript, and colours were used for symbolic significance or because they looked good. By the Renaissance a new study of anatomy became important in order to present the human figure as it really was. People were being depicted as individuals, not as types, which was the medieval way. Colour was used realistically and the revived interest in the Classical world was about creating a perfect state or beauty. Architecture produced ideal settings for this new society, just as painting might inspire a sense of greatness for the sitter and a feeling of purity for those looking at the painting. Leon Battista Alberti's book on Painting of 1435 said, 'We should consider it a very great gift to men that painting has represented the gods they worship.' He suggested that painting has contributed considerably to the piety which binds us to the gods, and to filling our minds with 'sound religious beliefs.' After all, the arts could elevate mankind into higher thought.[14]

Like his father, Henry VIII spent a fortune on tapestries. In 1540 a team of craftsmen worked with silk, wool, silver and gold gilt threads on a set of tapestries for King Henry depicting *The Labours of Hercules*. As Hercules was a demi-god it was an apt collection for a god-like king. Henry VIII, by this date, was Head of the Church in England so it was most suitable for him to be identified with Greek and Roman demi-gods.

*The Triumph of Hercules* was created after cartoons (drawings) were made in the school of the great Renaissance artist Raphael. Henry VIII claimed that the Raphael tapestries were his absolute favourites. Considering that by 1547 Henry owned some 2,200 valuable pieces of art – including eighty-five portrait drawings by Hans Holbein, 550 drawings by Leonardo da Vinci, groups by Raphael and Michelangelo as well as Dutch, Flemish, German and French drawings from the sixteenth century – this was an enormous compliment and illustrates how Henry's agents moved throughout Europe always seeking new art purchases.

The tapestries show many feats by Hercules, following his labours as a demi-god in compartments arranged in three tiers with the figure of fame and the grotesques above. The drawings of Greek gods placed in various poses, in particular, interested Henry VIII. In the central tapestry Hercules is scantily clad, holding a club-like lion stick. He is very virile, bearded and muscular as he holds a planet and strangles a lion. He shoots a centaur with an arrow in another image and also grabs hold of a naked woman.

By 1542 King Henry was physically unlike Hercules. He weighed 300lb, suffered from ulcerated legs, severe headaches and fevers. At this time Katherine Howard had been arrested under suspicion of adultery with Thomas Culpepper who was half Henry's age and considered exceptionally handsome. Henry had his completed tapestries mounted on the walls of Hampton Court and Whitehall.[15] It is a little ironic that Henry's set of *The Labours of Hercules* was a duplicate of that owned by Pope Leo X, as Henry had recently made himself Head of the Church in England instead of the Pope.

Furniture also received the Renaissance treatment. Henry VIII possessed an oak and walnut writing desk which was embellished with ornamental motifs, and decorated with figures of Venus and Mars in armour, Helen of Troy, Paris and Cupid. It also has the coats of arms of Catherine of Aragon and Henry and messages of allegiance. This desk is kept in the V& A Museum in London and remains one of the rare pieces of luxury Renaissance furniture to survive from the early Tudor era. With attractive godly images and stories from Greek and Roman myth inscribed on it, such furniture shows Henry as a true Renaissance prince, educated and in possession of beautiful objects. It was a pity that he became such a narcissistic, neurotic and cruel monarch, and not particularly successful in marital love.

# Chapter 11

# The Commoner, Villages, Towns and Sex

Most of the issues highlighted in this book's opening chapters such as religious taboos and sex did apply to ordinary people as well as to the wealthier classes. By ordinary people, I mean those who dwelled in towns and country villages. The Church dictated morality and all issues sexual before and after The Reformation, albeit in a different way after The Reformation.

Protestantism was to become the established religion between 1540 and 1700. Before the reign of Edward VI it still resembled the Catholic Church as regards liturgy and the belief in transubstantiation. The reformed Church's puritan wing was active in bringing Christian ethics to a majority of ordinary homes. This was evident amongst the gentry and urban bourgeoisie, sanctifying holy matrimony and encouraging the family to serve as a partial replacement for the parish. Among the peasant and artisan classes, the community of neighbours had a large influence and control over family life. A growing censorious attitude about sin accompanied sixteenth-century religious changes. This led to a increased interference by Church authorities and by neighbours to make everybody conform to the new norms. In this way society was reset. There was little or no privacy either and so for ordinary people there was no escaping a *new* morality.[1]

During the early Tudor period much remained as it was during the medieval era. Henry VIII only really wanted to replace the Pope as head of the Church. He saw himself as the upholder of the true Catholic faith. He never wanted extensive reform although a number of his ministers, in particular Thomas Cromwell, did desire religious change. When Henry died, the Church of England was a Catholic Church and followed a Catholic liturgy, even though monasteries were dissolved, a move that presented social consequences and lined King Henry's coffers. The English Church became thoroughly Protestant under Henry's son, the boy king, Edward VI, but his older half-sister Mary reversed it making

England Roman Catholic once again. His other half-sister, Elizabeth I was interested in a Protestant Church, but she was not a zealot and was initially flexible in her search for a middle way.[2]

Celebrations linked to the liturgical year in Catholic England always presented great opportunity for members of the opposite sex to meet and enjoy a little freedom. There were lesser-known festivals existent in the countryside which were never celebrated widely. A rush-bearing festivity, for example, was celebrated in Cheshire, Derbyshire, and Lancashire, all of which were regions important for producing mats, floor coverings and rush lighting.

After the break with Rome the number of festivals in England was reduced. Since they were holidays, banning many saints' days and festivals was advantageous for land owners and crafts businesses in towns. There was a determination on the part of the merchant class to make society more productive and this had an effect on everyday life. Christmas celebrations changed. This was a time when communities celebrated together. On Christmas Day three masses were said, the genealogy of Christ was sung and everyone in church held lighted tapers. Not everyone attended all three services and after the initial one people returned home for the first unrestricted meal in the four weeks since Advent. Twelve days of thorough enjoyment followed, opportunity for the sexes to intermingle through feasting, games and dancing, and a resumption of sexual activity despite most of the holiday period containing saints' days. The three main days of celebration were Christmas Day, New Year's Day – which followed the Roman calendar as the true New Year began on 25 March – and Epiphany or Twelfth Night.[2] Twelfth Night may have begun with an early morning church service but it ended with feasting and dancing and the opportunity for courtship.[3]

Christmastide wassails provided a socially acceptable festive drinking opportunity. Tudors enjoyed socialising in ale houses, which were always busy and would, on occasion, be frequented by mixed sex groups. Inebriation wasn't the preserve of the lower-classes, however. At the Field of the Cloth of Gold, ladies of the English court were observed passing a large wine flask and large cups 'which circulated more than twenty times' between themselves and French lords until they were drunk.

St Valentine's Day was celebrated in the fifteenth century and is mentioned in the Paston Letters of the 1470s. The poet Geoffrey Chaucer was the first to record St Valentine's Day as a day of romantic celebration in his poem *Parliament of Foules*, writing, 'For this was sent on Seynt Valentine's Day/ when every fool cometh ther to choose his mate.' It was believed in France and England that 14 February was the beginning of the birds' mating season. Valentines seem to have been chosen by a group of friends who had to buy their Valentine a gift. In the household of William Petre, a steward's accounts show gold trinkets and lengths of cloth being presented to Valentines chosen by lot. A maid who drew Sir William himself as a lot was given an extra quarter's wages as a gift.

Shrove Sunday, the seventh Sunday before Easter, was the last opportunity for fun before the Lent fast when yet again certain foods were forbidden, as indeed was sex. Shrove Tuesday was celebrated with entertainments such as plays, music and dancing which generally grew rowdy. Once the Lenten period began in February all rowdiness was supposed to stop as well as sexual activity. In churches the altar and lectern would be clothed over during Lent and a veil was hung separating the chancel and nave until Easter. Holy Week began with Palm Sunday when yew and willow were blessed as protection against evil. Relics were processed around the outside of the church and the laity would walk in their own procession before entering the church. The Lenten veil was drawn up and lowered again but by Easter it remained open.

By the sixteenth century towns held processions in honour of St George's Day. Guild members processed through towns with model dragons or statues of St George. By 1530 this became a day of national celebration. Easter and St George's Day brought out not only the hope of better weather but good times socially, offering opportunity for male-female encounters.

The largest building in any small town or village was the church though communal feasts tended to take place close by or in barns. May Day, for example, was a much-loved celebration of the summer warmth returning. Young people often 'made the May' by going to nearby woods where they collected greenery while wearing garlands of flowers. There are numerous bawdy songs associated with Maying which was a celebration religious reformers loved to criticise. The reformer, Philip Stubbs wrote later in the century, 'I have heard it credibly reported by men of great gravitie and reputation that of forty, three score, or a hundred maids going to the woods overnight. There has been scarce a third part of them undefiled.' The illegitimate birth rate for nine months henceforth does not give credence to his exaggeration. The busiest time for conceiving was actually later in summer.

At Whitsun unmarried young women of the town followed processions that included a statue of the Virgin. Corpus Christi was a popular summer festival in which rival parishes competed and put on Biblical plays which varied in complexity from place to place. However, the festival of Corpus Christi was abolished during the 1570s.

Midsummer, the feast of St John, was a thrilling time involving bonfires and various local traditions. In London, for example, up to 4,000 people would take part in what was known as 'watching marches' with displays of model giants, Morris dancing and pageants. Wakes occurred in late summer and early autumn. These were feast days celebrating the dedication of parish churches. Wakes would be marked with communal entertainments and dates would be staggered so that neighbouring parishes could entertain each other. These festivities could get so out of hand that Henry VIII restricted them to the first Sunday in October, which also helped to curb the number of holidays. Church ales were fundraising events held during the summer months which also involved much eating and drinking. Philip Stubbs considered these times of 'gluttony and drunkedness'.

The Harvest Home celebration saw the last sheaf of corn harvested. Men, women and maid servants rode through the streets in a cart shouting until they arrived at the barn for the Harvest Home supper. Hallow-tide was designed to help souls through purgatory. After evensong church bells would be rung to comfort the dead in purgatory and churches were illuminated with candles.

May Day dancing, Lords of Misrule on Twelfth Night and other much-loved traditions survived most of the sixteenth-century religious changes but gradually declined and often disappeared completely during the following century. By the end of the sixteenth century the gap between rich and poor had widened and the number of landless people was increasing. People became nervous of large gatherings such as Maying which was thought, in theory, to lead to illegitimate births which would consequently become a burden on the parish.

\* \* \*

Single and married women were at this time legally under the authority of fathers and husbands. They could not hold public office, make legal contracts or head a business. Widows, however, were different. They often ran businesses, especially in towns, until Henry VII curbed women's freedoms as sole traders in order to provide work for soldiers after the civil wars of the fifteenth century. This move unfortunately pushed many female sole traders out of business.

By the late sixteenth century fewer women worked as independent business women. A rise in prosperity and technological advances allowed markets to grow and capital available for larger scale investment pushed many craftswomen aside. During the early part of the era new opportunities were taken up by men, especially in traditional female crafts such as the silk industry and in brewing.[4]

Widows could remarry whomever they wished and they also could be extremely well off having inherited the widow's third part of inheritance, and even more if they were London City widows. It should be pointed out that in aristocratic circles widows were urged to remarry with hardly any time to grieve. Widows also enjoyed a hidden market value, particularly if their husbands had been established in a livery company. A second husband, should she choose to remarry, could hope to succeed to the first husband's position, not only in her bed but in her previous husband's livery company. Thus an apprentice could skip the remaining years of his apprenticeship in one deft move. He might have been her husband's right-hand man and understood the trade well. If the husband had grown ill the apprentice probably carried the burden of his trade.

After a long day's work the ale house was an attractive proposition. Ale house customers were generally men drawn from the poorer end of society, but poorer women did on occasions appear in ale houses, usually in family groups or with husbands and friends, as they were, in general, not considered respectable places for women to visit alone. Courting couples, though, might meet in the ale house while in company with others. Later in Tudor times those in authority were concerned about women entering an ale house where drunkenness could get out of hand, gambling might be rife and couples might indulge in sexual behaviour openly. Obvious drunkenness was generally frowned upon by all levels of Tudor society and considered detrimental to family prosperity. Even so, ale houses thrived as an important aspect of Tudor socialising and as an integral part of Tudor working life.[5]

*   *   *

As mentioned previously, marriage was deemed binding once the contract was agreed between the parties involved rather than when the church ceremony actually took place. In lower class families couples appear to have felt free to sleep together once the contract was agreed, which may explain the low illegitimate birth rate at the time (2–4 per cent).[6]

Adultery was not taken lightly. Many cases came before church courts and adulterers would be punished. A cheap printed paper from the era includes a ballad *How a Bruer meant to make a Cooper Cuckhold*.[7] In this popular ballad a wife hides her lover, a brewer, beneath an upturned tub to conceal him from her husband, a cooper. She tries to disguise the noises of protest and prevent her husband from looking beneath the tub, claiming to have trapped a pig under it. Verses in the ballad refer to different types of pig as a sexually overactive animal that wallows in filth. The brewer is eventually located under the tub, and a financial settlement is agreed between the parties.

This ballad is filled with innuendo and might have been enjoyed in the ale house amongst mixed company. Another popular ballad called *Watkin's Ale* emphasises the aggressive nature of a sexual victory a man has over a wife.[8]

Ballads served a number of purposes. They could be exciting, pass on news or relay religious and political views. They were printed with cheap woodcut illustrations and stuck up on walls as decoration. They were so popular, in fact, that Tudor monarchs tried to control them. Henry VIII issued the first proclamations banning offensive ballads in 1533 and again in 1542. Edward VI and Mary also exercised control over their publication. A licensing system was not set up until Elizabeth I's reign. In 1557 the Stationer's Company was granted its charter. All printers, except the Crown printers and the university presses, had to be members of the London companies and copies of all printed matter was supposed to be entered on the company's register. This was provided proof that the item was licensed and proof of the publisher's copyright.[9]

Many poems, songs, jokes and stories about sex circulated amongst Tudor society but they did not generally translate into unfettered sexual behaviour. Accusations of whoredom could end up in court on slander charges. Anyone convicted of adultery or sexual transgressions were forced to undergo public shaming rituals such as kneeling at church in front of the whole congregation wearing nothing but their underwear and holding a lighted taper. This occurred in addition to frequent corporal punishments. All sexual activity outside of marriage was condemned by the Church,[10] but as we have seen repeatedly, there were double standards in the Tudor world.

In an adult lifespan of thirty years there was a chance of being accused of fornication, adultery, buggery, incest, bestiality or bigamy. Half of the charges made were ill-founded, but if even half were true this would suggest a society that was frequently sexually lax, highly inquisitorial and all-too ready to denounce other's sins. Malice and backbiting were common characteristics of village society. There was a high level of extra-marital sex available everywhere, in town and country, despite punishments if the parties concerned were discovered. Many of the cases recorded were between maidservants and fellow servants or maids and masters of the house.[11] This is perhaps unsurprising as there was overcrowding in bedrooms. The maid often slept in the same bed as the master and mistress of the house. Foreign visitors to London during this time noted with shock how much freedom people had, men and women. In 1499 Erasmus remarked on the custom of greeting with a kiss on the lips suggesting that Englishwomen had far more freedom than their Continental contemporaries.

Employers might treat maid servants as social equals. For example, there is the story of a maid servant who minded her master's children and while they 'sported about' in Finsbury Fields she met a long-lost cousin, so claimed, and brought him back with her to her employer's house. Her mistress welcomed him, providing good cheer and inviting him to stay the night. On the next day all her silver had vanished.[12]

Several categories of bastardry occurred during the Tudor era according to court records. The first was the seduction of a girl by a fellow servant or worker, or even a neighbour, possibly after vague promises of marriage. The second type was the seduction of a living-in maidservant by a person of higher social status in position of authority over her. This might happen either with or without a promise of marriage. Obviously the servant might be afraid of losing her job and gave her consent. If the girl became pregnant all promises could be ignored and she was either discharged or married off to a poor man who would accept her and her prospective child. Thirdly, there was the alleged promiscuous girl, likely to be scorned and repudiated by the community, who had difficulty identifying the father.

The low level of pre-marital conceptions did not necessarily mean low levels of sexual activity for frustrated youths. Sex was readily available to rural bachelor youths who were encouraged to get a little experience before marriage (double standards once again). Towns had brothels, which were illicit but active, or certain ale-houses after Henry VIII closed down the stews. In the countryside some poor families let out a room in their house to a prostitute and the occasional married woman might indulge in fornication in the fields to earn money. In towns apprentices used and abused women especially on Shrove Tuesday just before Lent when sex was forbidden.[13]

One thing we really do know about marital sexual activity amongst the poor is that it fluctuated from month to month. There was a trough in conceptions during March and another during August and September. The period of most conception was April to July. The reason could be a taboo on sexual intercourse during Lent, and there was an absence of marriages during Lent. There may also have been greater privacy for couples once warmer weather arrived. Reduced sexual activity could also be due to physical exhaustion at harvest time, mid-summer and the separation of families due to migrant labour during the harvest period. Doctors advised sexual abstention during the heat of summer but it was unlikely that the poor listened to them. Besides, the poor rarely if ever saw a doctor.

\*   \*   \*

A huge change in the lifestyle of the upper classes as the sixteenth century progressed was an increasing desire for personal privacy and over the course of the next century large houses were built with corridors. During the Tudor era great houses with interlocking rooms remained the norm. The only way of moving around was by passing through other people's rooms. Sexual privacy was therefore almost impossible for any person of standing who wanted to have an affair. Servants spying through cracks in panelling, peering through keyholes, listening for creaking beds and inspecting bed linen for tell-tale stains was a usual occurrence. As for the poor, they lived in one- or two-chambered houses or in cramped cottages cheek by jowl. Privacy for the Tudor citizen, rich and poor, was a practical impossibility. Bundling often was sometimes the norm, especially during bitterly chill weather when adults would share a bed, even if not married. It was common to bundle in inns, and a maid might share a bed with a master and mistress. But no sex permitted, and night caps were worn to keep out devils as well as providing warmth, and the shift worn to deter straying hands.

Beds came in all shapes and sizes and materials too. They could be sacks of straw on raised sleeping platforms. They could be rush matting or simple rope-strung truckle beds on wheels that could be moved out of the way during the day or placed beneath larger bedsteads. Mattresses could be of hay, flock, wool or feathers. Some had only blankets as coverings but the more fortunate enjoyed sheets, pillows, bolsters and coverlets. Four posters might have wooden ceilings called testers. Others had cloth tops. These more elaborate beds cost dearly. Those owned by the nobility with four-post testers, silken hangings, many mattresses, linen sheets and luxurious coverings could be worth the same as a small farmer's lands.

Most country folk made do with a wooden bedstead and a flock mattress. Labourers and servants slept on floor mattresses if they were fortunate enough to be even raised off the floor where rats and mice scuttled about at night. Many of the landless might have a loose pile of straw on an earthen floor. Loose straw could work its way into layers of clothing and splinters caused problems for the skin. Straw in a sack made a lumpy bed unless diligently shaken daily. Bedstraw got its name from plants such as Lady's Straw stuffed into the sack's stuffing or into a mattress. *Galium verum*, a family of plants used for stuffing amongst the straw, might aid sleep as it helped deter insects, especially body fleas and lice.[14]

For the rising middle class the Renaissance introduced the fork, the handkerchief, and the nightdress. The Renaissance humanist believed in civility and external habits set apart the civilised from the uncivilised. Gradually, as the Tudor era continued, rather than sharing communal dishes and dipping in cutlery that had just been in one's mouth, a host would have a plentiful supply of plates, knives and spoons.[15] This aimed to separate one's body juices and odours from contact with other people in an effort to acquire privacy in many aspects of personal behaviour and moreover observe civility.

The world view before the sixteenth century for all people was that individuals in society were bound together in the 'Great Chain of Being'.[16] The purpose of life during the medieval era and into the sixteenth century, including sex, was the continuation of family, village or state, and not to consider the wellbeing of the individual. Personal preference, ambition and greed were subordinated to the notion of the common good. By the sixteenth century each individual was beginning to think of themselves as unique.

Societal change is slow, especially for ordinary people. It was not until the seventeenth century that nearly all human beings would consider themselves unique and therefore free to pursue their own happiness provided they respected the rights of others. 'Man was now freed to seek his own personal pleasure in the here and now, no longer hedged in by the narrow boundaries laid down by moral theology or traditional custom.'[17] It wasn't until the late sixteenth century that Protestant theology considered that sex could be for purposes other than procreation and that the sexual act could be considered as equally an important feature of marriage as the procreation of children.

# Chapter 12

# Naughty Vocabulary during the Tudor Era

'Language is fluid and malleable; it drives social attitudes rather than simply expressing them.' Kate Lister writes these words in her book *A Curious History of Sex*.[1] In this chapter I shall tell you some of the expressions and sexy quirks of language used during the Tudor period and into The Elizabethan era which could be heard on the streets of English towns. Some of the vocabulary used then is still used today though the connotation suggested by past usage was not always the same.

In *The Passionate Pilgrim*, a collection of poems in part written by Shakespeare, we find these lines:

> The wiles and giles that women work
> Dissembled with an outward show
> The tricks and toys within them lurk
> The cock that treads them shall not know.

We can read cock as a euphemism for a husband who is the victim of his cheating hen. Two things stand out as regards terminology associated with the spoken and written word. The misogynistic attitude to women as overly sexed creatures was ingrained into society and sex-related vocabulary used during the sixteenth century. Secondly, where alleged female adultery is concerned, as Michael Macrone comments in *Naughty Shakespeare*, 'a man deceived is a man whose beliefs are destroyed, whose reputation is shattered and whose progeny is now in doubt.'[2]

Sexual innuendos and language used during the Elizabethan period would have been commonplace for earlier Tudors. In Shakespeare's plays there are many suggestions of female adultery. The language used to express this appears to be without filter. For instance, in *Othello* we have 'A horned man's a monster and a beast.'[3] Othello may either take revenge or he can kill his wife by strangulation as Iago suggests. The sentiment written in the play clearly reflects society's attitudes, not just late Elizabethan society but that of earlier Tudor society. Humiliated men, cuckolded men, were viewed as impotent and foolish. Spectators would laugh at the victim and the word 'cuckold' might be thrown at him. Or he might be called 'wittol' or 'contented cuckold'.

Cuckold comes from the old French for cuckoo, the bird that lays eggs in other birds' nests. The cuckold might grow invisible horns marking a wife's infidelities and horn was often slang used for the erect penis. This is how we get the expression horny. Humiliation might lead a cuckolded man to 'horn-madness'. In *The Merry Wives of Windsor* Mister Ford can hardly escape shame in Act V. The horn-mad man in Shakespeare turns out to be a fool. If a wife strays there is not much a husband can do, and worry could drive a husband mad. Therefore, horn-madness is a male disease.[4]

Shakespeare's jealous men also reflect the Tudor age. They perceive wives and children as property. Their property is an extension of themselves. Adultery is not just theft, it is akin to a spiritual violation.

Tudors liked punning with words. I particularly enjoy these lines from *A Midsummer Night's Dream*.

Moonshine: "This lanthorn doth the horned moon present."

Demetrious: "He should have worn the horns on his head."

Theseus: "He is no crescent and his horns are invisible within the circumference."[5].

The mechanicals put on a play featuring the personified moon, horned because it is crescent-shaped and the word 'horn' is used as a pun here.

Another word used for horn is bugle. Baldrick is its belt, invisible as the horn it holds, as Benedick says in *Much Ado About Nothing*: 'That a woman conceived me, I thank her; that she brought me up, I likewise give her humble thanks; but that I will have a rechate winded in my forehead or hang my bugle in an invisible baldrick, all women shall pardon me.'[6]

The word whore comes from the Old Norse 'hora' meaning adulteress and was (and is) a term of abuse. It shames women by stigmatising their sexuality. The thirteenth-century definition of a whore was 'any woman who had sex outside of marriage'. This term was used to attack those who upset the status quo, usually as the male attempt to reassert sexual control and dominance over women. An accusation of 'whore' in the early Tudor era affected a woman's value on the marriage market. Using it lightly and foolishly meant the one using it could end up in front of the courts for slander. Most Tudor slander cases were brought by women who felt their good name was being questioned. Isobel Stone of York brought a suit against John Newbald for calling her 'a whore, a common whore and a piss-arsed whore.' Reputation was everything.[7]

The word cunt is easily several thousand years old. 'Cu' is associated with the Latin *cunnus* which means vulva and is the oldest word for vagina in the English language. Cunt was occasionally called pudding bag. Vulva dates to the late fourteenth century from the Latin word for womb. In a Latin dictionary of 1538 the vulva was defined as 'the womb or mother of any female animal.' While cunt was a bawdy word, it was not offensive. Grope Lanes or Cunt Lanes existed in many medieval cities.[8]

Medieval parents called their children cunts and it shows up in medieval surnames such as Godwin Clawecunte or Robert Clevecunt.[9] Medieval and Tudor society was not squeamish or offended by many terms we might consider offensive, although there were plenty of societal rules around sex. *Ragionamenti della Nanna e della Antonia* by Pietro Antonio (1534–1538) contains the line: 'Speak plainly, and say fuck, cunt and cock otherwise thou wilt be understood by nobody.'[10] Sex was a source of great humour, as Shakespeare observed, and eroticism or, at least, the thought of it. Sex was, of course, central to married life. Chaucer used the word 'cunt' in the *Canterbury Tales*, regarded by the Tudor court as the best of English literature. Another word often used was 'queynte' which means both knowledge and cunt. Queynte pops up frequently in Shakespeare.

Malvolio in *Twelfth Night* examines the handwriting in the note he discovers by his employer's box hedging. He fancies Olivia to be in love with him. It was a trick played on him, but he reads: 'There be her very Cs, her Us, and her Ts and this makes she her great Ps.' The line is a pun on cunt and piss both. Pamphlets and books with sexually obscene material were not censured until 1580 so the first century of printing had a free rein on language and suggestion. As sex became more repressed words linking to the body became taboo so that by the seventeenth century cunt had achieved a shock factor.[11]

The clitoris has been much ignored in past times because it provides female sexual pleasure. The translation of Arabic texts into Latin led to new terms for the clitoris. They include 'nymph', 'myrtle', 'tentigo' and 'virgo', the latter two alluding to an erection. The word 'bobrelle' in fifteenth-century Britain meant something raised, bobbing up and down.

'Quimberry' was used for the clitoris in *De Re Anatomica* in 1559. Both Realdo Columbo and Gabrielle Fallopio claimed discovery of the clitoris during the sixteenth century. Columbo claimed it produced a lady sperm called '*Amor Veneris*'. It was Renaissance anatomists who emphasised the clit's role in sex and pleasure. On the down side, Renaissance doctors suggested the clitoris could provide excess libido in women, with health and morality problems attached. An overused clit might morph into a penis which could be used by a woman to penetrate other women.[12]

\* \* \*

Language on the street was less restrained than that used in literature and poetry. Private manuscripts were often openly sexual in terminology. There is talk of shameful sex in these writings such as weak women 'giving way' and of women having 'no ability to control themselves when faced with male desire'. Society actually believed both sexes gained pleasure from sex and thought an orgasm was essential for a woman to conceive. Society considered also, as stated previously, that sexual misbehaviour was worse when committed by women than by men. Whilst a man could boast about his powers and his sexual appetite, a woman had to find extenuating circumstances to downplay her choice of actions.[13]

A list of sexual insults used in everyday street talk by Tudors includes the words whore, harlot, knave and bawd, which were often used in an aggressive manner. Smell-socks was a term to make fun of one who might sniff a woman's underwear. Euphemisms for sex included 'bed-sport', 'tilling the fields of Venus', or 'nice play' to suggest male and female enthusiasm. Ballads and jokes included a range of slang terms such as 'pie', 'secret parts', 'corner', 'plum', 'hole' or 'pond' for the vagina, and 'shaft', 'pride', 'tool', 'cock', 'prick and 'horn' for the penis. Prostitutes were whores, harlots, trulls, jills, drabs, and geese or mackerel. 'To make a fist' was a term meaning to masturbate as well as throwing a punch.[14]

Here is a further selection of naughty terms that existed in Tudor times from *Naughty Shakespeare*.

Assail/assault: laying siege to a body's chastity.

Bawdry: reference to the sex act. Bawdry is dirty talk or behaviour and the bawdy-house is the whore house.

Bone-ache: pain due to a venereal disease or the disease itself.

Cliff: take her cliff is slang for female parts such as clef.

Cock: actually also a substitute for God. 'Cock's passion' in *Taming of the Shrew*, IV. i. 118.

Codpiece: a man's privies as well as the decorative bag fashionable men like Henry VIII wore.

Die: to have an orgasm.

Do: all-purpose word for 'have sex'.

Drab: a prostitute.

Fig: expletive accompanied by an obscene gesture.

Jakes: privy or outhouse.

Lap: crotch.

Maidenhead: female virginity.

Malady of France: the pox.

Male varlot: masculine whore.

Naughty: lewd.

Pap: nipple.

Pistol or Pillicock: penis.

Play: to sport wantonly.

Powdering tub: a heated tub in which one was supposed to sweat a venereal disease.

Pox: venereal disease usually syphilis.

Privates: secret parts

Punk: low-class strumpet.

Quean: whore.

Stand to: be erect.

Stones: male part.

Thing: sex organ, male or female.

Tool: penis.

Top: satisfy a lover.

Treasure: a woman's sexual zone especially a virgin's sexual zone.

Tub-fast: abstinence from food and drink while in the powdering tub.

Tup: mating.

Virgin knot: hymen.

Weapon: male organ in an aggressive state.

Will: sexual desire but also referring to sexual organs.

Yard: penis.[15]

\* \* \*

During medieval and Tudor times, street names in towns reflected the work done there. For example, Love Lane may reflect a euphemism for prostitution occurring there. London's Love Lane was formerly Roper Lane, so named for the rope making business or after someone with the surname 'Roper'. Lovat Street was thought a corruption of Lucas, a local landowner, but it was formerly Love Lane and was changed to avoid confusion with London's other Love Lane. Stew Lane was named after the former stew or hot steamy bath that existed on premises there. Grope or Cunt Lane was common in towns. The meaning of the word grope was to clasp hands or grab. It has not significantly changed its meaning to this day.

Grope Lanes can be found in many English towns of the era such as Norwich, Bristol, York, Shrewsbury, Whitby, Wells, Newcastle and others. These lanes were narrow, dark alleys or passageways rather than actual streets. They were usually close to a town's commercial centre, close to market places, high streets or public quays, or near churches. This raises the question: did travellers and clergy as well as perhaps parishioners routinely resort to prostitutes?[16]

In Oxford Cocks Lane appears to be a place of illicit sex. In *Piers Plowman* by William Langland there is a reference to 'Clarisse of Cokkes Lane.' Like many other towns of the era, Cambridge hosted traditional fairs. The Stourbridge Fair lasted for a full month and sold luxury and everyday items. However, behind the tempting booths, one might discover equally appealing purpose-built bedrooms. During the fair streets would assume temporary names. One such street was named Oyster Row. Either oysters could be purchased there or sex, or, enticingly, both: 'they (hawkers) mingled with the poorest of the fair's customers and the rag-tag assortment of beggars, petty thieves and prostitutes also hoping to make their way.' The Cambridge Stourbridge Fair attracted many sex workers during the early 1500s and prostitutes would move between fairs.[17]

Perhaps the next time you are in one of the above mentioned cities you might keep an eye out for sexually explicit names reaching back centuries and indicative of places where, during the sixteenth century, a needy man, priest or youth might seek sex. Next time you watch a Shakespeare play do consider the saucy language he used – commonplace in Tudor society – as euphemism or when punning, explicitly sexual and very often sexist to our twenty-first century, liberated ears but also titillating and very entertaining.

# Conclusion

This book has been a joy to research and write. Tudor times are very distant for us. They not only contain amazing stories of sex and love but these tales are interesting and indicative, too, of a period of great societal change. Not only was there a new ruling family in power in 1485, one that strove to establish itself after Henry VII was crowned King of England, the Tudor era was the beginning of a more modern age influenced by enlightened Renaissance thought. Many previously held beliefs were gradually eroded during the first half of the sixteenth century, such as the days the Church insisted were not sanctioned for sexual encounter. While the Protestant religion was establishing itself in England, many superstitions around childbirth, though often comforting, gradually faded away. Equally, there were not so many opportunities for villagers to enjoy secret courtships or sneaky sex once various church feast days were abolished. Meanwhile, monks and nuns were cast out of monasteries and nunneries, some later marrying. However, the village community of shutter snitches, key-hole peepers and other watchers continued into the next era and beyond. Perhaps it is not simply a case of history repeating but, rather, human nature.

Procreation was essential if the Tudor dynasty was to survive. Elizabeth of York was fortunate in that she gave birth to male children who lived. Sadly, Arthur Tudor did not live long enough to be his father's successor though he was married briefly to a beautiful princess. We shall never really know if he and Catherine of Aragon slept together and that remains one of English royal history's great secrets. What a controversy and what permanent change emerged after that particular divorce. One would think Henry VIII might have known if Catherine was virginal when they married in 1509 but chose later not to.

The romantic and sexual stories attached to King Henry VIII's court and those of his unfortunate wives could leave a reader horrified and relieved not to be living there at that time. That Henry's two daughters became queens in their own right is a testament to a change for women's independence during this era. No woman in England had been a queen in her own right before, though many medieval queens were successful consorts and many were left in charge of the kingdom when their husbands were abroad or their sons were too young to rule.

Researching the oldest profession, treatments for the newly discovered syphilis, abortion, contraception, cosmetics, costumes and dance was intriguing. It amazed me to discover the cleverness and degree of sexual and romantic symbolism in the art of the Renaissance period. Many of the great houses and palaces we know today were founded during this era. While these provided more privacy in various closed rooms and parlours than had previously existed in a manor house or castle, maids could be easily seduced and women more easily hidden away in domesticity to be designated their husband's helpmate and support. It was also a time of great families and courtiers who climbed the greasy pole to position at court. The middle class was increasingly rising to great wealth and importance at this time. Merchants imitated nobility and found new ways to gain local political power, particularly in the City. Thomas Cromwell was a perfect example of a middling sort who achieved great power during the 1530s, reminding us that those who rose high could fall just as easily from royal favour.

Researching festivals, courtship and the private lives of ordinary folk such as the lavenders and wise women is fascinating. For them, too, change was unfolding. No longer did the monastery or nunnery edge onto a village or exist in towns. No longer was there an extra support system in place for the poor. In time there would be Poor Laws. Priests could marry after The Reformation and a parson might be up for grabs as possible reliable husband material. And though, for many people, daily life continued as it had during the late medieval era, most folks must have been confused by many of the religious changes which impacted on their spiritual sense of existence: changes to worship such as the liturgy observed and a reliance on saints to facilitate prayer. They may have felt uplifted to have a Bible in English placed in every parish church, but for most it would be a very long time before they could read it.

Tudor weddings, accompanied by drums and fiddles and the noise of happy laughter, are always delightful for a writer to investigate. No marriage was complete without consummation and it was consummation that made the marriage legal. Every antic on a wedding day led to the *act*. At a wedding, the atmosphere was full of sexual jokes and suggestion. It was a time, too, when the hand-fasted marriage was still recognised and observed, although it was not so usual as hand-fasting was dying away. Church marriage was firmly in vogue.

Legislation concerning sex changed during the period. There was the Buggery Act introduced by Thomas Cromwell in 1532. There was the Brothel Legislation of the 1540s. There was the beginning of a series of acts condemning witchcraft which impacted on many village wise women. And, crucially, there was the Reformation and the many acts passed in the name of this major religious and societal change.

The Tudor period was an era of great beauty, with exquisite gardens owning secret arbours and mazes and banqueting houses, all places where lovers could secretly meet. Poetry written during the Tudor era was incredibly clever but also sad, full of unrequited sexual suggestion and romantic love. Romantic and sexual ballads sung in villages had been sung for centuries and would continue to be sung.

The mores and traditions associated with sex, love and marriage may inevitably evolve, but sex and sexuality remain part of what it is to be human.

# Endnotes

## Chapter 1

1. Locke, Hilary Jane, *Chivalry and Courtly Love: Cultural Shifts, Gender Relations and Politics in Early Tudor Court Culture*, Academia, University of Adelaide.
2. Singer, S.W. (ed), The life of Anne Boleigne in *The Life of Cardinal Wolsey*, 1825.
3. Shulman, Nicola, *Graven with Diamonds, the many lives of Thomas Wyatt*, Short Books, 2011, pp90–91.
4. Ibid, p92.
5. Ibid, pp92–93.
6. Tannahilly, Realy, *Sex in History*, Stein and Day Publishers, NY, p137.
7. 1 Corinthians, 6, 15–16, *New English Bible*.
8. Stone, Lawrence, *The Family, Sex and Marriage in England, 1500–1800*, Penguin, 1977, p34.
9. Byson, Sarah, *Sexual Intercourse in Tudor Times*.
10. Stone, Lawrence, p34.
11. Ibid, p309.
12. Goodman, Ruth, *How to be a Tudor. A Dusk to Dawn Guide to Everyday Life*, Penguin Random House UK, 2015, p13.

## Chapter 2

1. Goodman, Ruth, *How to be a Tudor*, Viking, 2015, pp263–267.
2. Worsley, Lucy, *If Walls could Talk*, Faber & Faber, 2011, pp63–64.
3. Ibid, p69.
4. Lindsey, Karen, *Divorced, Beheaded, Survived*, De Capo Press, 1995, P.145, p150.
5. Vele, Abraham, *The Deceyte of Woman*, Early English Books, 1560, accessed through quod.lib.umich.edu.
6. Cressy, David, *Birth, Marriage & Death*, Oxford University Press, 1999, p285.
7. Ibid, pp234–260.
8. Leyser, Henrietta, *Medieval Women*, Phoenix Press, 1995, pp115–117.
9. Cressy, David, p269.
10. Ibid, p271.
11. Ibid, p277.
12. Sim, Alison, *The Tudor Housewife*, Sutton Publishing, 1998, p11.
13. Ibid.

14. Houlbrooke, Ralph A, *The English Family* 1450–1700, London and New York, Longman, 1984, p78.
15. Delony, Thomas, *The Pleasant History of Jack Newbury*, Clarendon Press, Oxford, 1912, p22.
16. Ibid.
17. Sim, Alison, p96.
18. Ibid, p97.
19. Worsley, Lucy, p69
20. Translated by Burgess, G and Busby K, *The Lais of Marie de France*, p66.
21. Angsar, Henry, Dershowitz, Alan M, *The Matrimonial Trials of Henry VIII*, Wipf and Stock, 2004, pp203–4.
22. Lister, Kate, *A Curious History of Sex*, Unbound, 2020, p84.
23. Coyne Kelly, Kathleen, *Performing Virginity and Testing Chastity in the Middle Ages*, Routledge, 2000, pp28–31.
24. Lister, Kate, p87.
25. Ibid, p89.
26. Green, Monica H, ed. *The Tortula*, Penn Press, 2001, p103.
27. Ibid.
28. Leyser, Henrietta, *Medieval Women*, Phoenix Press, 1995, p110.
29. Lister, p127.
30. Ibid.
31. Leyser, Henrietta, p116.
32. Ibid.
33. Whatley, William, *A Bride Bush or A Direction for Married Persons Planely Describing the Duties Common to Them and Peculiar to Each of Them*, Thomas Mann, 1619, p15.

## The Bedding Ceremony

1. Bartholomew, *De Proprietatibus Rerum*, 1535, Book IV.
2. Bartholomew, 1535, Book VI.
3. Borman, Tracy, *The Private Lives of the Tudors*, Hodder, 2017, p19.
4. Ibid.
5. License, Amy, In Bed with the Tudors, Amberley Publishing, 2013, Kindle Books, p13.
6. Ibid, p18.
7. The Rutland Papers, ed. By William Jerdan, *Original Documents Illustrative of the Times of Henry VII and Henry VIII, Camden Society*, 1842.
8. Borman, Tracy, *The Private Lives of the Tudors*, p21.
9. Ibid, p22.
10. Hall's Chronicle, p425.
11. Borman, Tracy, *The Private Lives of the Tudors*, p26.
12. Ibid, p23.
13. Ibid.
14. License, Amy, *In Bed with the Tudors*, p55.

15. Borman, Tracy, *The Private Lives of the Tudors*, p56.
16. Ibid, pp56–57.

**Chapter 3**
1. Weir, Alison, *Henry VIII*, *King and Court*, Jonathan Cape, 2001, pp403–408.
2. Weir, Alison, *Jane Seymour, The Haunted Queen*, *Author Notes*, Headline Review, 2018, p511.
3. Hartnell, Jack, *Medieval Bodies, Life, Death and Art in the Middle Ages*, Profile Books, 2018, p241.
4. Cressy, David, *Birth, Marriage & Death*, pp60–63.
5. Ibid, p65.
6. Hartnell, Jack, *Medieval Bodies*, p242.
7. Hartnell, Jack, *Medieval Bodies*, pp231–232.
8. Weir, *Henry VIII*, p139.
9. Lister, Kate, *A Curious History of Sex*, p50.
10. Ibid.
11. Lister, Kate, p164.
12. Hartnell, Jack, *Medieval Bodies*, p25.
13. Ibid, p15.
14. Ibid, p234.
15. Ibid, p235.
16. Cressy, David, *Birth, Marriage & Death in Tudor and Stuart England*, p197.
17. Ibid, p199.
18. Ibid, p200.
19. Cressy, David, p204.
20. Latimer, Hugh, *Sermons by Hugh Latimer*, ed George Elwes Corrie, Parker Society; Cambridge, 1844, p336. {Cressy, P.207, what does this refer to?}.
21. Lister, Kate, *The Curious History of Sex*, p269.
22. Finch, B.E. and Green, Hugh, *Contraception through the Ages*, Peter Owen, London, 1963, p22.
23. Ibid, p100.
24. Finch and Green, *Contraception through the Ages*, p100.
25. Stone, Lawrence, *The Family, Sex and Marriage in England* 1500–1800, Penguin, 1979, p308.
26. Ibid.
27. Bryson, Sarah, https:// www.tudorsociety.com/childbirth-in-medieval-and-tudor-times-by-sarah-byson
28. Hartnell, Jack, *Medieval Bodies*, p140.
29. Ibid, p259.

*A Summary of Tudor Childbirth Beliefs*
1. Licence, Amy, *In Bed with the Tudors*, Amberley Publishing, 2012, pp29–33.
2. Ibid, p33.

3. Ibid.
4. Ibid, pp213–215.
5. Raine, James, *Fabric rolls of York Minster*, quoted in B.Rowland *Medieval Woman's guide to Health*, University of Kent, 1981 and in Licence, Amy, p215.
6. Brown, Petrina, *Sex, Childbirth and Motherhood through the Ages*, Summerdale Press, 2003.
7. Licence, Amy, *In Bed with the Tudors*, pp217–218.

**Chapter 4**
1. Goodman, Ruth, *How to be a Tudor*, Viking, 2015, p26
2. Worsley, Lucy, *If Walls Could Talk*, Faber & Faber, 2011, p108.
3. Goodman, Ruth, p19.
4. Lister, Kate, *A Curious History of Sex*, Unbound, 2020, p242.
5. Russells, John, *The Boke of Nature*, Project Gutenburg, http://www.gutenburg.org, pp66–67.
6. Lister, Kate, p 236.
7. Mazzo Karras, Ruth, *Common Women, Prostitution and Sexuality in Medieval England*, Oxford University Press, 1998, p54.
8. Goodman, Ruth, p19.
9. Ibid, p23.
10. Ibid, pp31–33.
11. Ibid, p34.
12. Lucy Worsley, p85.
13. *Recettario Novo Probatissimo a Molte Infirmita, E Etiandio Di Molte Gentilezze Utile A Chi Le Vora Provare* (Venice 1532).
14. Lister, Kate, p243.
15. Ibid, p244.
16. www.dictionary.com.
17. Goodwin, Ruth, *How to be a Tudor*, p39.
18. Ed and trans. Monica H. Green, *The Tortula*, Penn. University Press, pp45–47.
19. Goodwin, Ruth, *How to be a Tudor*, p35.
20. Medievalists.net. *Did people in the Middle Ages take baths?*
21. Boraccio, *Decameron*, 1972, trans. by McWilliam, G.H Harmondsworth, Penguin.
22. Capgrave, John, 1999, *Life of St Katherine*, Winstead, K.A. (ed) TEAMS. Kalamazoo, MI: Medieval Institute Publications.
23. Archibald, Elizabeth, *Bathing, Beauty and Christianity in the Middle Ages*, *Insights*, Durham University, Institute of Advanced Study, Vol 5, 2012, Number 1.

**Chapter 5**
1. Simei Synman, Irene, *The True Nobility of Self Fashioning in the 16thCentury*, accessed via Academia.

2. *The Tudor Treasury*, Carlton Publishing Group, 2014, pp33–36.
3. Worsley, Lucy, *If Walls Could Talk*, p145.
4. Goodwin, Ruth, *How to be a Tudor*, p48.
5. Lister, Kate, *A Curious History of Sex*, p287.
6. Glover, Michael, *Thrust, A Spasmodic Pictorial History of the Codpiece in Art*, David Zwirner Books, p6.
7. Glover, Michael, p7.
8. www.Lucyworsley.com.
9. Synman, Irene, Simei, *The True Nobility of Self Fashioning in the 16th century*, accessed via Academia.
10. *The Tudor Treasury*, p36.
11. Goodwin, Ruth, *How to be a Tudor*, p67.
12. Ibid, p81.
13. Worsley, Lucy, *If Walls Could Talk*, p139.
14. Ackroyd, Peter, *Dressing Up, The History of an Obsession*, Thames and Hudson, 1979, p27.
15. Stow, John, *A Survey of London, Written in the Year 1598*, The History Press, 2005, p99.
16. Ackroyd, Peter, p71.
17. Ibid.
18. Maczelika, Csaba, *Cross Dressing in Early Modern England*, University of Szeged, accessed in Academia.
19. *Mundus alter et idem*, attributed to Joseph Hall, 1605. Amazon, Create Space Independent Publishing, 2010, Latin., Yvronia tributa, in suas partes, pxxx,{page no} *The Discovery of a New World*, translated by John Healey, 1937, Harvard University Press.

### Tudor Dance and Music

1. Sim, Alison, *Pleasures and Pastimes in Tudor England*, Sutton Publishing Ltd., 1999, p99.
2. Thoinot Arbeau, *Orchesography*, tr., Mary Stewart Evans, Dover Publications Inc., New York, 1967, p11.
3. *Tudor Dances and Dance Forms*, http:// www.elizabethenglandlife.com.
4. Sim, Alison, p102.
5. Ibid, p105.

### Chapter 6

1. Ives, Eric, *The Life and Death of Anne Boleyn*, Blackwell Publishing, 2010, p69.
2. Shulman, Nicola, *Craven with Diamonds*, p138.
3. Norbrook, David, editor, *The Penguin Book of Renaissance Verse*, p17.
4. *The Penguin Book of Renaissance Verse*, selected by Norbrook, David, ed by Woudhuysen, H. R., Penguin, 2005, p185.
5. Irish, Bradley J, *Gender and Politics in the Henrician Court*, accessed via Academia.

6. Ives, Eric, *The Life and Death of Anne Boleyn*, p72.
7. Ibid, p73.
8. Shulman, Nicola, *Graven With Diamonds*, Short Books, 2012, pp142–145.
9. Irish, Bradley J, *Gender and Politics in the Henrician Court*, Academia.
10. Ibid..
11. Shulman, Nicola, *Graven with Diamonds*, p188.
12. Ives, Eric, *The Life and Death of Anne Boleyn*, p72
13. *Penguin Book of Renaissance Verse*, P.181. http//www.interestingliterature. com. *The Best Sir Thomas Wyatt Poems Everyone Should Read.*
14. Shulman, Nicola, p190.
15. Ibid, p199.
16. Ibid, p208.
17. Ibid.
18. Penguin Book of Renaissance Verse, p182.
19. Shulman, Nicola, p110.

**Chapter 7**
1. Fraser, Antonia, *The Six Wives of Henry VIII*, Mandarin, 1992, P.130., cit Ridley, *letters* , p37.
2. Ives, Eric, *The Life and Death of Anne Boleyn*, Eric Ives, Blackwell Publishing, 2010, p189.
3. Ibid, p87.
4. Ibid, p63.
5. Ibid, pp64–65.
6. Ibid.
7. Guillaume de Lorris, *The Romance of the Rose*, trans. Frances Hogan, 1999, Oxford World Classics.
8. Shulman, Nicola, *Graven With Diamonds*, Short Books, 2012, p175.
9. Ibid, p180.
10. Weir, Alison, *Henry VIII*, Jonathan Cape, 2001, p380.
11. Ives, Eric, The Life and Death of Anne Boleyn, p299.
12. https://www.science20.com/news_articles/henry_viii_and_miscarriages_ was_it_kell_antigen-76877
13. Ives, Eric, *The Life and Death of Anne Boleyn*, p327.
14. Ibid, p329.
15. Ibid, p344.
16. Ibid, p340.

*Court Mistresses*
1. Watkins, Sarah Beth, *The Tudor Brandons*, Chronos Books, 2016. Chapter Four.
2. Borman, Tracy, *The Private Lives of the Tudors*, Hodder, 2016, p88.
3. Ibid, p133.
4. Ibid, p134.

5. LP, Henry VIII Vol VI Part ii, nos. 1018, 1054.
6. Borman, Tracy, *Private Lives of the Tudors*, p159.
7. Ibid, p161.
8. Ibid, pp158–159.

**Chapter 8**
1. Stone, Lawrence, *The Family, Sex and Marriage in England*, p314.
2. Ibid, p323.
3. Ibid, p315.
4. Lister, Kate, *A Curious History of Sex and Sexuality*, p310.
5. Ibid, p321.
6. Ibid, p233.
7. Langham, William, Barker, Christopher, *The Garden of Health*, London, 1579, p147.
8. Lister, p237.
9. Ibid.
10. http://www.tudornation.com/thestews, accessed 6 August 2020.
11. Snow, John, *Survey of London*, p345.
12. http://www.mapoflondon.uvic.ca, card 3, accessed 6 August 2020.
13. Stow, John, *Survey of London*, p345.
14. *The Regulation of Brothels in Late Medieval England*, http://www.jstor.org/stable/3174556, accessed 7 August 2020, pp3–4.
15. Ibid, pp14–15.
16. CLRO, Rep. 3, Fol 157v-158v; Letter Book N, fol. 47v.
17. *The Regulation of Brothels in Late Medieval England*, p14.
18. Alighieri, Dante, *The Divine Comedy*, Vol.!, Inferno, Canto V trans by Mark Musa, London, Penguin Books, 1971, p10.
19. Haynes, Alan, *Sex in Elizabethan Times*, Sutton Publishing, p65.
20. Ibid, p62.
21. St Thomas Acquinas, Summa Theologae Vol. 20: *Pleasure*, ed. By E.D'Arcy, London: Eyre & Spottiswoode, 1975, p65.
22. Weisner, Merry E, *Prostitution and the Question of Sexual Identity in Medieval Europe*, Journal of Women's History, II.2, 1999, p61.
23. Blomefield, p739.
24. History Today, *Contemporary Accounts of the Perils, Pleasures and Growing Pains for Young English Women in the Late Middle Ages*, 45.6, 1995, pp25–33.
25. *Annals of Cambridge*, p76.
26. Kavanagh, Helen, *The Topography of Illicit Sex in Later Medieval English Provincial Towns*. https:pure.royalholloway.ac.uk/portal/files/37318718/2020KavanaghHMphil.pdf. accessed 9.9.2020. p72.
27. Ibid, p93.
28. The Questioning of John Rykener, *A Male Cross-Dressing Prostitute*, 1395; Internet Medieval Sourcebook, 1998. <http://wwww.fordham.edu/halsall/source/ 1395rykener.asp.

*Aphrodisiacs and Love Potions*
1. Shah, J, Erectile Dysfunction Through the Ages, DJU International, 90.4, 2002, p433.
2. Notchesblog.com, what was the ultimate medieval aphrodisiac? accessed 28.08.2020.
3. Ibid.
4. Evans, Jennifer, *Aphrodisiacs, Fertility, Medicine* in Early Modern England.
5. Lister, p163.
6. Ibid p151.
7. Ibid.
8. Haynes, Alan, *Sex in Elizabethan England*, Sutton Publishing, 1997, p70.
9. http//www.bbc.co.uk., The Sweet Makers: A Tudor Feast, accessed 28.08.2020.
10. History Extra.com., *love potions*, accessed 28.08.2020.
11. Ibid.
12. Williams, Slattery, *BBC History Revealed*, February 2020, accessed 28.08. 2020.

**Chapter 9**
1. Ives, Eric, *The Life and Death of Anne Boleyn*, pp297–298.
2. Stone, Lawrence, Family, *Sex and Marriage*, Penguin Books, 1990, p309.
3. Berkowitz, Eric, *Sex and Punishment, 400 years of judging desire*, The Westbourne Press, 2012, p156.
4. Kramer, Heinrich, *Hammer of the Witches*, trans. By Montague Summers, 1928, Introduction.
5. Lamb, Victoria, *Witchcraft in Tudor Times*, History Today, 15.08.2012.
6. englandcast.com, hteysko@gmail.com, 20.10.2015, accessed 29.06.2020.
7. Tudorplace.com.ar., *Witchcraft and Magic*, accessed 29.06.2020.

**Chapter 10**
1. Hughes, Bethany, *Venus/ Aphrodite*, Weidenfield & Nicolson, 2019, pp75–82.
2. Stott, Deborah, *Style and Theory in Renaissance Reliefs*, Bunting Institute Colloquium, 1983, p9.
3. Borman, Tracy, *Thomas Cromwell*, pp52–53.
4. Open University, *Art and Visual Culture: Medieval to Modern*, pp8–12.
5. Woodall, Joanne, *Portraiture*, Manchester University Press, St Martin's Press, p4.
6. Ibid p7.
7. Ibid, p16.
8. Hughes, Bethany, *Aphrodite/Venus*, p159.
9. Ibid.
10. Ibid, p173.
11. Nichols, Dr Chelsea, *The Museum Weirdo*, www.ridiculouslyinteresting. com, accessed 18.08.2020.

12. Ibid.
13. Ibid.
14. Sim, Alison, *Pleasures & Pastimes in Tudor England*, Sutton Publishing, 1999, p5.
15. Bilyeau, Nancy, www.nancybilyeau.blogspot.com, *The Strange and Beautiful World of Tapestries*, 3 May 2015, accessed 18.08.2020.

Chapter 11
1. Stone, Lawrence, *The Family, Sex and Marriage*, 1500–1800, Penguin Books, 1977, p105.
2. Sim, Alison, *Pleasures & Pastimes in Tudor England*, Sutton Publishing, 1999, pp75–76.
3. Ibid, pp77–93.
4. Stone, Lawrence, *Family, Sex and Marriage*, p110.
5. Goodman, Ruth, *How to be a Tudor*, HB, Penguin Books, 2015, p182.
6. Cressy, David, *Birth, Marriage & Death in Tudor and Stuart England*, Oxford University Press, 1999, p277.
7. Goodman, Ruth, *How to be a Tudor*, p273.
8. Ibid, p274.
9. Sim, Alison, *Pleasures and Pastimes in Tudor England*, p127.
10. Goodman, Ruth, *How to be a Tudor*, p274.
11. Stone, Lawrence, *Family Sex and Marriage*, pp324–345.
12. Picard, Liza, Elizabeth's London, Phoenix, 2004, p201.
13. Stone, Lawrence, p390.
14. Goodman, Ruth, How to be a Tudor, p10.
15. Stone, Lawrence, p171.
16. Ibid, p172.
17. Ibid, p159.

Chapter 12
1. Lister, Kate, *A Curious History of Sex*, p7.
2. Macrone, Michael, *Naughty Shakespeare*, Ebury Press, 1998, p135.
3. Ibid, *Othello*, IV,i. L.62.
4. Ibid, p136.
5. Ibid, *A Midsummer Night's Dream*, V. i. 240–42.
6. Ibid, *Much Ado About Nothing*, 1.i. 238–42.
7. Lister, Kate, accessed Inewes.co.uk, opinion, 7 June 2018.
8. Lister, Kate, *A Curious History of Sex*, p21.
9. Ibid.
10. Ibid.
11. Ibid, p25.
12. Ibid, p50.
13. Goodman, Ruth, *How to be a Tudor*, p270.
14. Ibid, p273.

15. Macrone, Michael, *Naughty Shakespeare*, pp181–208.
16. Holt, R & N.Baker ed by L.Bevan, *A Geography of Sexual Encounter: Gender in English Medieval Towns, Indecent Exposure: Sexuality, Society and Archaeological Record*, Fife: Cruithe Press, 2001, pp201–216, 210–213.
17. VCH, *A History of Cambridgeshire and the Isle of Ely*, III, p92.

# Bibliography

Ackroyd, Peter, *Dressing Up, The History of an Obsession,* Thames and Hudson, 1979.

Ackroyd, Peter, *Tudors, The History of England*, Volume II.

Alighieri, Dante, *The Divine Comedy*, Vol.!, Inferno, Canto V trans by Mark Musa, London, Penguin Books, 1971.

Angsar, Henry, Dershowitz, Alan M, *The Matrimonial Trials of Henry VIII*, Wipf and Stock, 2004.

Archibald, Elizabeth, *Bathing, Beauty and Christianity in the Middle Ages, Insights,* Durham University, Institute of Advanced Study, Vol 5, 2012, Number 1.

Bartholomew, *De Proprietatibus Rerum*, 1535, Book IV.

Berkowitz, Eric, *Sex and Punishment, 400 years of judging desire*, The Westbourne Press, 2012.

Bilyeau, Nancy, www.nancybilyeau.blogspot.com, *The Strange and Beautiful World of Tapestries*, 3 May 2015, accessed 18.08.2020.

Borman, Tracy, *The Private Lives of the Tudors*, Hodder, 2017.

Borman, Tracy, *Thomas Cromwell*, Hodder, 2015.

Bryson, Sarah, https:// www.tudorsociety.com/childbirth-in-medieval-and-tudor-times-by-sarah-byson

Boraccio, *Decameron*, trans. by McWilliam, G.H Harmondsworth, Penguin, 1972.

Brown, Petrina, *Sex, Childbirth and Motherhood through the Ages*, Summerdale Press, 2003.

Capgrave, John, 1999, *Life of St Katherine*, Winstead, K.A. (ed) TEAMS. Kalamazoo, MI: Medieval Institute Publications.

Cohen, Jenny, *Did Blood Cause Henry VIII's madness and Reproductive Woes?* http.//www. History.com. updated 1 September 2018.

Coyne Kelly, Kathleen, *Performing Virginity and Testing Chastity in the Middle Ages*, Routledge, 2000.

Corinthians, 6:15–16, *New English Bible*.

Cressy, David, *Birth, Marriage & Death*, Oxford University Press, 1999.

Delony, Thomas, *The Pleasant History of Jack Newbury*, Clarendon Press, Oxford, 1912.

Evans, Jennifer, *Aphrodisiacs, Fertility,* Medicine in Early Modern England. englandcast.com, hteysko@gmail.com, 20.10.2015, accessed 29.6.2020.

Finch, B.E. and Green, Hugh, *Contraception through the Ages*, Peter Owen, London, 1963.

Glover, Michael, *Thrust, A Spasmodic Pictorial History of the Codpiece in Art*, David Zwirner Books.

Goodman, Ruth, *How to be a Tudor. A Dusk to Dawn Guide to Everyday Life*, Penguin Random House UK, 2015.

Grace Book B, Part II: *Containing the Accounts of the Proctors of the University of Cambridge, 1511–1644*, ed. By Mary Bateson, Cambridge University Press, 1905.

Green, Everett, *Lives of Princesses of England from The Norman Conquest*, Vol 5

Green, Monica H, ed. *The Tortula*, Penn Press, 2001.

Guillaume de Lorris, *The Romance of the Rose*, trans. Frances Hogan, 1999, Oxford World Classics.

Hartnell, Jack, *Medieval Bodies, Life, Death and Art in the Middle Ages*, Profile Books, 2018.

Hall's Chronicle

Haynes, Alan, *Sex in Elizabethan Times*, Sutton Publishing, 1997.

History Today, *Contemporary Accounts of the Perils, Pleasures and Growing Pains for Young English Women in the Late Middle Ages*, 45.6, 1995.

Holt, R. & Baker, N. ed by Bevan, L., *A Geography of Sexual Encounter: Gender in English Medieval Towns, Indecent Exposure: Sexuality, Society and Archaeological Record*, Fife: Cruithe Press, 2001.

Houlbrooke, Ralph, A, *The English Family* 1450–1700, London and New York, Longman, 1984.

Hughes, Bethany, *Venus/Aphrodite*, Weidenfield & Nicolson, 2019.

Ives, Eric, *The Life and Death of Anne Boleyn*, Eric Ives, Blackwell Publishing, 2010.

Kramer, Heinrich, *Hammer of the Witches*, trans. By Montague Summers, 1928.

Kavanagh, Helen, *The Topography of Illicit Sex in Later Medieval English Provincial Towns*. https:pure.royalholloway.ac.uk/portal/files/37318718/2020KavanaghHMphil.pdf, accessed 9.09.2020.

Lamb, Victoria, *Witchcraft in Tudor Times*, History Today, 15. 8. 2012.

Latimer, Hugh, *Sermons by Hugh Latimer*, ed George Elwes Corrie, Parker Society; Cambridge, 1844.

Lawless, Erin, *Forgotten Royal Women, The King and I*, Pen & Sword, 2019.

Leyser, Henrietta, *Medieval Women*, Phoenix Press, 1995.

License, Amy, *In Bed with the Tudors*, Amberley Publishing, 2013.

Lister, Kate, *A Curious History of Sex*, Unbound, 2020.

Locke, Hiliary Jane, University of Adeliade, *Chivalry and Courtly Love: Cultural Shifts, Gender Relations and Politics in Early Tudor Court Culture*, Academia.

LP, Henry VIII Vol VI Part ii, nos. 1018, 1054.

Macrone, Michael, *Naughty Shakespeare*, Ebury Press, 1998.

Maczelika, Csaba, *Cross Dressing in Early Modern England*, University of Szeged, accessed in Academia.

Mazzo Karras, Ruth, *Common Women, Prostitution and Sexuality in Medieval England*, Oxford University Press, 1998.

Medievalists.net. Did people in the Middle Ages take baths?

Mumby, *The Youth of Henry VIII, A Narrative in Contemporary Letters*.

*Mundus alter et idem*, attributed to Joseph Hall, 1605, Create Space Independent Publishing, 2010, Latin., Yvronia tributa ,in suas partes, *The Discovery of a New World*, translated by Healey, John, 1937, Harvard University Press.

Nichols, Dr Chelsea, *The Museum Weirdo*, www.ridiculouslyinteresting.com, accessed 18.08.2020.

Norbrook, David, editor, *The Penguin Book of Renaissance Verse*, 2005.

Notchesblog.com., what was the ultimate medieval aphrodisiac? Accessed 28.08.2020.

Nichols, Dr Chelsea, *The Museum Weirdo*, www.ridiculouslyinteresting.com, accessed 18.08.2020.

Open University, *Art and Visual Culture: Medieval to Modern*.

*Recettario Novo Probatissimo a Molte Infirmita, E Etiandio Di Molte Gentilezze Utile A Chi Le Vora Provare* (Venice 1532).

Rowland, B, *Medieval Woman's guide to Health*, University of Kent, 1981.

Shah, J, *Erectile Dysfunction through the Ages*, DJU International, 90.4, 2002.

Shulman, Nicola, *Graven With Diamonds*, Short Books, 2012.

Sim, Alison, *Pleasures & Pastimes in Tudor England*, Sutton Publishing, 1999.

Sim, Alison, *The Tudor Housewife*, Sutton Publishing, 1998.

Singer, S.W. (ed), The life of Anne Boleigne in *The Life of Cardinal Wolsey*, 1825.

St Thomas Acquinas, Summa Theologae Vol. 20: *Pleasure*, ed. By E.D'Arcy, London: Eyre & Spottiswoode, 1975.

Stone, Lawrence, *The Family, Sex and Marriage*, 1500–1800, Penguin Books, 1977.

Stott, Deborah, *Style and Theory in Renaissance Reliefs*, Bunting Institute Colloquium, 1983.

Stow, John, *A Survey of London, Written in the Year 1598*, The History Press, 2005.

Synman, Irene, Simei, *The True Nobility of Self Fashioning in the 16th century*, Accessed via Academia.

Tannahilly, Realy, Sex in History, Stein and Day Publishers, NY, 1980.

*The Lais of Marie de France*, translated by Burgess, G and Busby K.

The Questioning of John Rykener, *A Male Cross-Dressing Prostitute*, 1395; Internet Medieval Sourcebook, 1998. <http://wwww.fordham.edu/halsall/source/ 1395rykener.asp.

*The Regulation of Brothels in Late Medieval England*, http://www.jstor.org/stable/3174556, accessed 7 August 2020.

The Rutland Papers, ed. By William Jerdan, *Original Documents Illustrative of the Times of Henry VII and Henry VIII, Camden Society*, 1842.

The Sweet Makers: A Tudor Feast, http//www.bbc.co.uk. accessed 28.08.2020.

*The Tudor Treasury*, Carlton Publishing Group, 2014.

Thoinot Arbeau, *Orchesography*, tr., Mary Stewart Evans, Dover Publications Inc., New York, 1967.

*Tudor Dances and Dance Forms*, http://www.elizabethenglandlife.com.

Vele, Abraham, *The Deceyte of Woman*, Early English Books, 1560, accessed through quod.lib.umich.edu.

VCH, *A History of Cambridgeshire and the Isle of Ely*, III.

Weir, Alison, *Henry VIII, King and Court*, Jonathan Cape, 2001.

Weir, Alison, *Jane Seymour, The Haunted Queen*, Headline Review, 2018.

Weir, Alison, *Anna of Kleves*, Headline, 2018

Watkins, Sarah Beth, *The Tudor Brandons*,

Weisner, Merry E, *Prostitution and the Question of Sexual Identity in Medieval Europe*, Journal of Women's History, II.2, 1999.

Whatley, William, *A Bride Bush or A Direction for Married Persons Planely Describing the Duties Common to Them and Peculiar to Each of Them*, Thomas Mann, 1619.

Worsley, Lucy, *If Walls Could Talk*, Faber & Faber, 2011.

Woodall, Joanne, *Portraiture*, Manchester University Press, St Martin's Press.